Snapshots

A Collection of Readings for Adults

CAMBRIDGE Adult Education
Prentice Hall Regents, Englewood Cliffs, NJ 07632

Executive Editor:	Brian Schenk
Developmental Editor:	Marjorie P.K. Weiser
Project Editor:	William J. Bennett, Jr.
Production Manager:	Arthur Michalez
Managing Editor:	Eileen Guerrin

Cover Photographs by Marc Anderson
Cover Design by Dick Granald, L.M.D. Studios

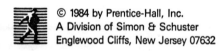
© 1984 by Prentice-Hall, Inc.
A Division of Simon & Schuster
Englewood Cliffs, New Jersey 07632

Printed in the United States of America

10 9 8 7 6 5 4 3

ISBN   0-8428-9550-7

Prentice-Hall International (UK) Limited, *London*
Prentice-Hall of Australia Pty. Limited, *Sydney*
Prentice-Hall Canada Inc., *Toronto*
Prentice-Hall Hispanoamericana, S.A., *Mexico*
Prentice-Hall of India Private Limited, *New Delhi*
Prentice-Hall of Japan, Inc., *Tokyo*
Simon & Schuster Asia Pte. Ltd., *Singapore*
Editora Prentice-Hall do Brasil, Ltda., *Rio de Janeiro*

CONTENTS

ACKNOWLEDGMENTS

The following have generously given permission to adapt or use extended passages from copyrighted works:

From *Me Quit Smoking? Why?* Copyright © 1975 by American Lung Association. Courtesy of American Lung Association.

Adapted from "Keeping Warm," *Low-Cost, No-Cost Energy-Saving Ideas,* © 1983. Reprinted through the courtesy of Consolidated Edison Company of New York, Inc.

From *Tally's Corner: A Study of Negro Street Corner Men.* Copyright © 1967 by Little, Brown and Company (Inc.). By permission of Little, Brown and Company.

Copyright © 1983 by The New York Times Company. Reprinted by permission.

Excerpts adapted from "Nancy Kincaid" from *Hillbilly Women* by Kathy Kahn. Copyright © 1972, 1973 by Kathy Kahn. Reprinted by permission of Doubleday & Company, Inc.

Copyright © 1984 by *USA Today.* Courtesy of *USA Today.*

From *Understanding Microcomputers* by Rose Deakin. Copyright © 1982, 1983 by Rose Deakin. Reprinted by arrangement with New American Library, New York, New York.

From the book, *Organizations, Clubs, Action Groups.* Copyright © 1980 by Elsie E. Wolfers and Virginia B. Evansen. Reprinted with permission of St. Martin's Press, Inc., New York.

"Bill Talcott" condensed by permission of Pantheon Books, a division of Random House, Inc. from *Working: People Talk About What They Do All Day and How They Feel About What They Do,* by Studs Terkel. Copyright © 1972, 1974 by Studs Terkel.

From *Selma, Lord, Selma,* by Sheyanne Webb, Rachel West Nelson, Frank Sikora. © 1980 The University of Alabama Press. Used by permission.

Adapted from "How Electricity is Made," *Using Electricity Safely in Your Home,* © 1977 by Con Edison. Reprinted by permission of Con Edison, New York.

Excerpted from the book *Preparing for Your New Baby,* by Shirley Camper Soman. Copyright © 1982 by Shirley Camper Soman. Reprinted by permission of Delacorte Press.

Adapted from *Not Working* by Harry Maurer. Copyright © 1979 by Harry Maurer. Reprinted by permission of Holt, Rinehart and Winston, Publishers.

Excerpts adapted from *Hard Living on Clay Street* by Joseph T. Howell. Copyright © 1973 by Joseph T. Howell. Reprinted by permission of Doubleday & Company, Inc.

"Hobart Foote" condensed by permission of Pantheon Books, a division of Random House, Inc. from *Working: People Talk About What They Do All Day and How They Feel About What They Do,* by Studs Terkel. Copyright © 1972, 1974 by Studs Terkel.

Adapted with permission of Macmillan Publishing Company from *A Stranger in the House* by Robert Hamburger and Susan Fowler-Gallagher. Copyright © 1978 by Robert Hamburger.

Excerpts adapted from *Blue Collar Women, Pioneers on the Male Frontier,* by Mary Lindenstein Walshok. Copyright © 1981 by Mary Lindenstein Walshok. Reprinted by permission of Doubleday & Company, Inc.

© 1982 by Phyllis Volkens. All rights reserved. Used by permission.

Andrew A. Rooney, Adapted from *A Few Minutes with Andy Rooney.* Copyright © 1981. Reprinted with the permission of Atheneum Publishers, Inc.

"America and I," by Anzia Yezierska, from *The Open Cage,* copyright © 1979, by Louise Levitas Henriksen. Reprinted by permission of Persea Books, Inc., 225 Lafayette Street, New York, N.Y. 10012.

Excerpt from *Liberated Parents/Liberated Children* by Adele Faber & Elaine Mazlish, © 1974 by Adele Faber and Elaine Mazlish. Reprinted by permission of Grosset & Dunlap, Inc.

TO THE READER

SNAPSHOTS is an anthology put together for your reading enjoyment. The reading passages in this book have been selected to meet a wide range of adult interests. You will find articles on relationships, child care, health and fitness, money, computers, working—and not working—along with many other subjects. Most of these selections come from recent books, newspapers, and magazines. Many are written in the natural language used by real people in daily life. All deal with real concerns about living in today's world.

Each reading passage is followed by several multiple-choice questions. These questions will help you get the full meaning from each passage you read. In the back of the book, starting on page 89, you will find the answers to these questions. You will also find an explanation of how to use what's in the passage to find the correct answer. In answering the questions, use only information from the passage you have just read. Try not to use things you already know to answer the questions. You may have additional knowledge of some of the subjects discussed, but remember that the questions are based only on information in the passage.

You can use these questions and answers to measure your own reading skills. Each answer has a label that will tell you which skill the question was testing. Some questions will help you find the **main idea** in the passage. Others will guide you to the **supporting details** used by an author to build the argument or message. There are questions that will call on you to think about the connections among different statements in the passage. These are **inference** questions. They ask you to figure out an unstated idea from stated information. Other questions will help you reach a **conclusion.** You might, for example, have to figure out how one thing leads to another. You will also find questions about the **style** and **tone** of the passage: Is it humorous? Serious? Dramatic? Poetic? How did the author's words sound to you? How do you think the author wanted you to feel? There are also **vocabulary**-building questions for each passage. These questions will guide you to the meanings of unfamiliar words, or of phrases that are used in unusual ways.

Just for fun, there are some word puzzles and jumbles scattered throughout the book. And there are questions labeled **for discussion.** These call on you to think about what you have just read, and how it might connect to your life. Perhaps we should have labeled these discussion questions "food for thought." We hope they will give you ideas to talk over with people you know.

Most of all, we hope you enjoy *Snapshots: A Collection of Readings for Adults.*

The Editors

1

Remember the old days? Lots of people thought smoking was just a harmless habit. Maybe it was even good for your nerves.

Those days are gone forever. More than 30 million Americans have quit smoking. A hundred thousand of them are doctors. Do they know something you don't?

Just one cigarette does this:

- Lowers the temperature of your skin.

- Immediately upsets the flow of blood and air in and out of your lungs.

- Speeds up your heartbeat.

Cigarette smoke paralyzes the cilia. Cilia are tiny hairlike particles. They move about to help keep your lungs clean and ward off infection. You need them in good working order.

Smoking hurts at all ages. A study of youngsters (ages 11 to 18) shows more sickness among those who smoke. Another study shows that men (ages 40 to 69) who smoke are hospitalized 50 percent more often than non-smokers. Smoking is the chief cause of chronic bronchitis, lung cancer, emphysema.

The facts are grim. The risk of premature death from all causes is greater among cigarette smokers than among non-smokers. *A lot greater:*

- 1.7 times greater from coronary artery disease

- 6 times greater from bronchitis and emphysema

- 10 times greater from lung cancer

Some other statistics about cigarette smoking are given in the graphs on the next page.

But the risk doesn't have to be great if you quit smoking.

The minute you stop smoking, your body goes to work to repair the damage that smoking has caused. Your cough will

Some Facts About Smoking and Cigarettes

Number of cigarettes smoked per year (in billions):

500

610

Spending by cigarette industry to sell cigarettes (in millions of dollars):

$261.3

$1000

Lung cancer deaths per 100,000 women per year:

5.8

18

Percent of adults who smoke:

53%

38%

1964   1980

Sources: National Center for Health Statistics; Department of Agriculture

lessen or disappear. You will be able to breathe easier. You will feel less tired. Your circulation will improve. So will your sense of taste and smell. Your heart and lungs will have a chance to defend themselves against illness.

Your family and friends want you alive and well. Cigarettes won't keep you that way. Kick the habit. It's a matter of life and breath. □

Adapted from *Me Quit Smoking? Why?*, American Lung Association, 1975.

1. The main point that the author of the passage is trying to make is that the risk of

   (a) lung disease is greater for smokers than for non-smokers
   (b) premature death is greater for smokers than for non-smokers
   (c) cancer is greater for smokers than for non-smokers
   (d) premature death is greater for male smokers aged 40–69

2. The author would probably agree with the research that says that smoking

   (a) might be good for your nerves
   (b) is more dangerous to women than men
   (c) is a life-and-death issue   .
   (d) causes all of the lung cancer found in women

3. Which of the following words could be used in the place of "premature" in the sixth paragraph?

   (a) sudden   **(c)** painful
   (b) early   **(d)** expected

4 According to the passage, smoking just one cigarette will

   (a) slow your heartbeat
   (b) slow the flood of blood to your skin
   (c) speed up your heartbeat
   (d) kill the cilia in your lungs

5. The graph on page 2 says that fewer adults smoked in 1980 than in 1964, but more cigarettes were smoked in 1980. From the information in the graph, you can conclude that this happened because

   (a) more women smoked cigarettes
   (b) fewer adults got lung cancer
   (c) more low-tar cigarettes were made
   (d) fewer doctors smoked cigarettes

6. The word "paralyzes" in the third paragraph most nearly means

   (a) quickens   (c) moves
   (b) lowers   (d) stops

7. According to the graph, all of the following have increased since 1964 EXCEPT

   (a) deaths of women from lung cancer
   (b) the percent of adults who smoke
   (c) spending by the cigarette industry
   (d) number of cigarettes smoked per year

8. From the information in the passage, you can infer that once you stop smoking

   (a) you will live 20 years longer
   (b) your skin temperature gets lower
   (c) vou will not be hospitalized
   (d) your lungs begin to clean themselves

Check your answers on page 89.

9. **(For discussion)** Now you know some of the things that smoking does to your body. If you smoke, will knowing these things make you quit? Why or why not? If you have quit already, or if you never started, what made you decide to quit or not start?

More energy is used to heat homes than for any other purpose. There are often large spaces under doors through which cold air enters your home and warm air leaves. A closed tube of cloth filled with sand or some other dense substance is an effective way to block these openings. You can easily make such a draft guard to place at the bottom of your door.

Take an old sheet or shirt of tightly woven fabric. From it cut a strip several inches longer than the width of your door, and about 5 inches wide. (See Figure A.)

Fold strip in half lengthwise and sew along one short end and the long side. Leave the other short end open for turning and stuffing. (See Figure B.)

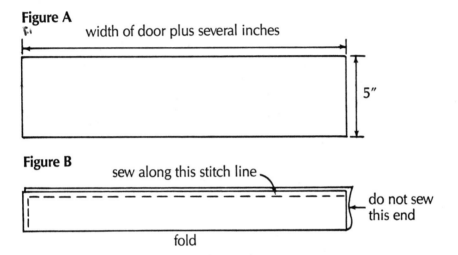

Figure A — width of door plus several inches — 5″

Figure B — sew along this stitch line — do not sew this end — fold

Now turn inside out. You should have a long tube. Fill with sand, and sew remaining end closed. Place on the floor to cover the space through which air has been escaping. You can make·one of these draft guards for every doorway through which cold drafts enter your home. □

Adapted from "Keeping Warm," *Low-Cost, No-Cost Energy-Saving Ideas*, Con Edison, 1983.

1. Which of the following would be the best title for the passage?

   (a) A Sewing Project
   (b) How You Can Re-use Old Rags
   (c) An Easy Energy Saver
   (d) How You Can Heat Your Home

2. According to figures A and B, when making the draft guard you should take the material and

   (a) fold in thirds and cut along one side
   (b) fold in half and sew down the center
   (c) cut it so it's more than 5" wide
   (d) cut it slightly longer than the width of the door

3. With which of the following statements would the author probably agree?

   (a) There is nothing you can do about big heating bills.
   (b) Buying a new house will save the most energy.
   (c) Spending a lot on heating bills is the best way to keep warm.
   (d) You can spend less money on heat and still stay warm.

4. Which of the following substances could be used instead of sand to make the draft guard?

   (a) paper   (c) feathers
   (b) gravel   (d) plastic wrap

5. According to the passage, you should NOT sew all sides of the tube before it is turned inside-out because the

   (a) tube must be filled before it is closed
   (b) fabric will tear when the tube is turned inside-out
   (c) tube must first be placed by the door
   (d) fabric is cut to the width of the door

6. From the information in the passage, you can conclude that the sand-filled tube saves energy because it

   (a) is about 5" wide   (c) fills up an opening
   (b) reflects cold air   (d) stores warm air

7 The word "effective" in the first paragraph most nearly means

    (a) fast   **(c)** strange
    (b) good   **(d)** strong

8. The tone of the passage sounds most like a

    (a) play   **(c)** novel
    (b) textbook   **(d)** speech

Check your answers on page 90.

9. **(For discussion)** The passage shows you one way to make something that helps save energy. But there are many others. Describe some that you may know about. Do you know how they're made? Draw a diagram to show how to make one.

>>>>>>>>> *3* >>

Lorena tried to cajole, tease, shame, encourage, threaten, or otherwise attempt to make her man a man. Lorena said that in the beginning of her marriage, she used to pray to God, "Make John a good husband and father." Then she realized that "that's not God's job, that's my job." She changed her prayers: "Lord, this is Lorena Patterson. You know all about me. You know what I need."

So Lorena took on herself the job of making John a good husband and father. But it didn't work. She blames herself for the failure of her marriage, but she blames John, too. John was a boy, she said, not a man. He wasn't the "master."

"I want the man to wear the pants, but John made me wear the pants, too. His pants had a crease in them. Mine had a ruffle, but I was wearing the pants, too." □

From *Tally's Corner* by Elliot Liebow. Boston: Little Brown & Co., 1967. P. 133.

1. According to the passage, Lorena would probably say that for a marriage to work out, the most important thing is that the

    (a) man must have a job
    (b) woman must pray to God
    (c) man must be strong and take charge
    (d) woman must take the blame for problems

2   Which of the following words could be used in place of the word "cajole" in the first line of the passage?

    (a) ignore   (c) cheat
    (b) coax   (d) joke

3. The first paragraph says that Lorena changed her prayers. From the information in the passage, you can infer that her new prayers asked God to

    (a) make John a good husband and father
    (b) make John realize everything was his fault
    (c) help Lorena forget her broken marriage
    (d) help Lorena to make John stronger

4. When Lorena uses the words, "His pants had a crease in them, mine had a ruffle," she means that she

    (a) didn't like to wear dresses
    (b) and John dressed alike
    (c) had to run the family
    (d) had pants that looked like John's

5. The word "otherwise" appears in the first sentence of the passage. There are many smaller words that can be spelled with the letters used in "otherwise." Can you find ten of them?

Check your answers on page 92.

6. **(For discussion)** Lorena wanted John to take charge and be the master of the house. Years ago, this was almost always the role a man played in a family. There are still many people who would agree with Lorena. But today, many people are taking different roles in families. Many more women have jobs. Family decisions are shared, not made by the husband alone.

What do you think caused these changes? What do you think about the new roles men and women are taking in society? What kind of marriage role is better for you?

To the Editor:

I read an article in your paper the other day that said that women stay with men who beat them because these women don't think very much of themselves in the first place. This is hogwash!

You stay because:

- Anywhere you can go, he can go. And when he finds you, he'll beat the tar out of you.

- He tells you that if you try to leave, he'll find your child and take it out on her. Or he threatens your parents, or even your pet.

- You lose your friends. You have no *place* to go. If someone does take you in, he'll follow you. And not many people can put up for long with his constant pestering. I learned this the hard way when a policeman told me that my violent husband was *my* problem. He said I had no right to bother the police with him.

- He lies well. You run away. What happens? He "explains" to the police that you are crazy and must be brought back.

• Doctors can't believe that such a nice, quiet guy would do the things you say he does. And of course, there are never any witnesses.

You got into this fix because you never thought a nice, quiet guy would beat you up. The first times he did it, his tears afterward made you feel like the whole thing was *your* fault. Maybe you didn't love or trust him enough. Later, when others agree that it was your fault, all you know is that you tried. And you couldn't get away.

I was lucky. I got away. But I still have bitter memories of the cops and doctors that said I must enjoy being hit, or else I'd leave.

(Name withheld) □

Adapted from a letter to the editor, *The New York Times*, December 20, 1983.

1. The author is most concerned with explaining why

   (a) men beat their wives
   (b) women marry men who beat them
   (c) women stay with men who beat them
   (d) beaten women have a bad opinion of themselves

2. The author gives all of the following as reasons why women stay with men who beat them EXCEPT that

   (a) the men are good liars
   (b) the police won't help
   (c) their children will be threatened
   (d) doctors can make the men stop

3. The author wrote her letter to the editor because she

   (a) wants men to feel guilty
   (b) enjoys writing about her problems
   (c) disagrees with what the newspaper said
   (d) wants to embarrass her husband

4. The author would probably agree with the statement that, to protect themselves, beaten women

    (a) can go to the police
    (b) need someplace to go
    (c) can count on their friends
    (d) should go to the doctor

5. The word "pestering" in the fifth paragraph most nearly means

    (a) bothering   **(c)** yelling
    (b) beating   **(d)** lying

6. From the information in the passage, you can infer that the author's name was not printed because she was

    (a) lying about her husband
    (b) afraid of her husband
    (c) playing a joke on her husband
    (d) no longer married to her husband

Check your answers on page 93.

7. **(For discussion)**   The author says that some people think that women often "enjoy being hit," or that violence in the home is always the woman's fault. Another belief is that when a woman is raped, she is "asking for it"; in other words, "it's her own fault." How are these two beliefs alike?

 **5**

How far can law-enforcement officers go to catch someone breaking the law? Should they be able to use any methods they want to investigate someone they think may be a criminal? The writers of the Constitution tried to find the answers to these questions. But as a country, we are still looking.

In 1979, the F.B.I. began a secret investigation. The people being investigated weren't bank robbers or mobsters. They were judges in the city of Chicago. After four years, some of the judges were accused of taking bribes. The F.B.I. is happy with the results. But the F.B.I.'s methods have raised questions again.

"We knew there were crooked judges," says a federal lawyer. "We knew it was a big problem here. So we used a big operation." The F.B.I. used a large number of agents on the operation. Every judge in the city was checked out. But out of 334 judges, only three were accused. Some of the doubt about the investigation comes from this fact. If only three judges were found to be dishonest, was the problem really so big?

Of greater concern, though, are some of the methods the F.B.I. used. The investigators bugged the judges' offices and recorded everything they said. Since most of the judges were honest, the F.B.I. heard only private meetings. These are an important part of a judge's job. Critics say that the Constitution forbids this kind of listening-in. They point to several Supreme Court decisions. The Supreme Court has said that the police must have a good reason to think that a person is breaking the law before using bugs and telephone taps.

Another method used in the investigation is also being criticized. The F.B.I. made up over 100 phony cases, with phony defendants. The "defendants" were F.B.I. undercover agents, and the cases were tried in the judges' courts. At some time during the trial the undercover agent would ask to see the judge in his office. Then he would try to bribe the judge. Almost all the judges refused, but the agents were persistent. When they failed, they would try again, and keep trying. Sometimes another agent would call the judge at home and try to convince him to take the bribe.

Some people call this "entrapment." Entrapment is illegal. The law says that a police officer cannot trap someone into committing a crime and then arrest him.

Some experts also say that filling the courts with phony "cases" isn't fair to the judges, or the public. "Putting in 100 or so sham cases seems to be tampering with the court," commented one lawyer in the city. Others point out that the courts in Chicago are already overcrowded with *real* cases.

The F.B.I. and the police are using more and more under-cover operations of this kind. When the investigations reveal drug smugglers or killers, official methods are rarely questioned. But sometimes honest citizens or good judges are seen to be treated like criminals. Then it is necessary to ask the question again: Did the police go too far? □

Based on "Questions About Methods Used in Chicago Court Investigation" by E. R. Shipp, *The New York Times*, December 19, 1983.

1. According to the passage, the F.B.I. accused some judges after investigating them for

   (a) 1 year   (c) 3 years
   (b) 2 years   (d) 4 years

2. According to the passage, before the police can use bugs and wire-taps, they must

   (a) change the Constitution
   (b) ask the Supreme Court
   (c) have a good reason
   (d) ask a judge

3. From the information in the passage, what can you conclude the F.B.I. agents were MOST concerned with when they investigated the judges?

   (a) supporting the law   (c) finding honest judges
   (b) making arrests   (d) bribing judges

4. According to the information in the passage, when the F.B.I. agents tried to bribe the judges in Chicago, the agents were

   (a) enforcing the law   (c) following orders
   (b) acting illegally   (d) finding evidence

5. The word "sham" in the fifth paragraph most nearly means

   (a) secret **(c)** fake
   (b) unfair **(d)** criminal

6. From the information in the passage, you can conclude that if more of the judges had taken the bribes from the F.B.I. agents

   (a) people wouldn't have been as critical
   (b) undercover operations would stop
   (c) people would still want more proof
   (d) judges in other cities would be investigated

7. From the information in the passage, you can conclude that the word "persistent" means

   (a) confused **(c)** sneaky
   (b) dishonest **(d)** stubborn

8. The author would probably agree with the statement that the best way for the F.B.I. to support the law would be to

   (a) never use bugs or wiretaps
   (b) act like crooks to catch crooks
   (c) always obey the law themselves
   (d) keep people honest by watching them

Check your answers on page 94.

9. **(For discussion)** The F.B.I.'s job is to uphold the law and serve the public. The passage tells you about a big investigation. Many agents were used. It probably cost the taxpayers a lot of money. Do you think the investigation was worth the money? Do you think the F.B.I. upheld the law and served the public? What could they have done differently?

6

I've worked all my life, I've done men's jobs, I've done everything. I've used screwdrivers, electric drills, and punch presses. I really know what it means to do man's work. What gets me is, you work all your life like a dog. You pay your taxes into these government programs. But still, when you need help, the people that are paid to help you, they act like it's coming out of their own pockets.

My husband George had a stroke not long ago. I've always worked all my life and I never had to do this before, but when George had the stroke I knew I needed some help. I had to quit my job to take care of him.

So I went down to the welfare and told them I needed help. We were living with my son at the time. The welfare people said that since we were staying there, he had to take care of us. If we wanted help, we'd have to move out. The trouble was we didn't have anything at all, and George was in the hospital.

When I knew I needed some help, I went up here to this place called Hub Center where they're supposed to help people. Well, I told this young kid that was working there that we were starving and didn't have the money to pay our rent or buy our medicine. Well, he started writing something down on a slip of paper, and he wrote for the longest time. Then he gave it to me and he said, "Take this paper to 1631 Vine Street and they'll give you a sandwich."

I said, "Thanks for nothing, kid."

I never was so embarrassed in all my life. I thought, well, I know I have to be going crazy. I just have to be, this just can't be happening. □

Condensed from "Nancy Kincaid," *Hillbilly Women* by Kathy Kahn. New York: Doubleday & Co., 1972.

1. The best title for the passage would be

    (a) I Really Know Man's Work
    (b) Applying for Welfare
    (c) Where Are They When You Need Them?
    (d) Where Do Our Taxes Go?

2. From the information in the passage, you can infer that the author thinks that the person at Hub Center was

    (a) lying to her
    (b) not really interested in her
    (c) cheating her
    (d) making fun of her problems

3. When the author goes to the welfare office, she needs help because she

    (a) wants to quit her job
    (b) wants to move out of her son's house
    (c) has to take care of George
    (d) can't get help at Hub Center

4. A "punch press" is most likely a

    (a) screwdriver   (c) factory machine
    (b) farm machine   (d) electric drill

5. From the information in the passage, you can conclude that the author couldn't get help from welfare because

    (a) she and her husband could still work
    (b) her husband was not really sick
    (c) her husband was still in the hospital
    (d) she and her husband lived with her son

6. From the information in the passage, you can infer that the author thought that she should get government benefits because she

    (a) was too old to work
    (b) had paid her taxes
    (c) had asked for them
    (d) was working in a factory

7. According to the information in the passage, the person at Hub Center filled out a form so that the author could

    (a) get welfare   **(c)** pay the rent
    (b) buy medicine   **(d)** get a sandwich

8. When the author talks about asking for help from the government her tone is

    (a) frightened   **(c)** lazy
    (b) desperate   **(d)** relieved

Check your answers on page 96.

9. **(For discussion)**   The author's husband was very sick. She was living with her son at the time her story takes place, so you can tell that she and George did not have a home of their own. When she went to Hub Center, she had no money for food or medicine. Why do you think she waited so long before asking for help? Do you think she could have saved herself some trouble by asking for help sooner?

10. **(For discussion)**   Our taxes pay for many different government services. If people pay all of their taxes, do you think they should receive all of the services the government can offer? Why or why not?

×××××××× *7* ×××

Carlos Arboleya came to the U.S. from Cuba in 1960. He had only $40 in his pocket and the clothes on his back.

"I hitchhiked the streets looking for a job," he said. He now heads fifty-one banks in south Florida.

It's the kind of "Horatio Alger" success story that Americans still believe in. According to a recent nationwide poll, 81 percent of the adults spoken to still believed in the American Dream. They said that they believed that even the poorest child can rise to riches.

Horatio Alger first sparked this belief with his "rags-to-riches" novels for boys. Alger died in 1899.

"There's no question. The American Dream is here for all of us," Arboleya says.

Some say women may be the newest success stories:

"The rags-to-riches story is beginning to take shape for them," said Azie Taylor Morton. She is the first black U.S. Treasurer.

Morton picked cotton in Texas, and became active in the civil rights struggle. She later worked for President Kennedy. She is now an executive for a Virginia computer company. Her advice: "Don't be afraid to explore. But don't be in a hurry to accomplish anything too fast."

Mary Kay Ash is another success story. She heads the Mary Kay Cosmetics company. The company earns over $1 billion a year. Ash started working at age 7. She cared for her sick father while her mother worked to keep the family.

Her company now employs more women making more than $50,000 a year than any other company in the country.

John W. Galbreath started as an Ohio farm worker. By working in real estate, he has become one of the richest men in the world. He's now 88, and he is still looking for challenges. "If you dedicate yourself and say, 'This is my life's work,' no one can stop you," he said.

For Laura Fan, a high school senior, the message is clear.

"If you put your mind to anything you want—you're going to get it," said Fan. She came to the U.S. from Taiwan. Her goals? She wants to be a lawyer and an ambassador to the United Nations.

"I know it will be hard. I'm a woman and a Chinese-American, so the odds are against me. But I'll give it my best shot." □

"We believe rags-to-riches success can be ours" by Carolyn Pesce. *USA Today,* January 13, 1984.

1. The main idea of the passage is that people who make the American Dream come true are

    (a) born poor like Horatio Alger
    (b) born in other countries
    (c) making $50,000 a year
    (d) hard workers who know what they want

2. According to the passage, the American Dream may best be described as

    (a) dreaming about money
    (b) going from rags to riches
    (c) working for a big company
    (d) becoming an American citizen

3. All of the following names have something in common EXCEPT

    (a) Carlos Arboleya   **(c)** Mary Kay Ash
    (b) John W. Galbreath   **(d)** Horatio Alger

4. With which of the following statements about success would the author most likely agree?

    (a) You need luck to be successful.
    (b) You must go to college to be successful.
    (c) You can take charge of your life.
    (d) You must be born in America to be successful.

5. From the passage you can conclude that the words "I'll give it my best shot" in the last paragraph mean

    (a) I'll probably fail
    (b) I'll try as hard as I can
    (c) I'll give up trying
    (d) I'll graduate from college

6. The style of the passage is most like a

    (a) speech   **(c)** play
    (b) newspaper   **(d)** novel

7. According to the information in the passage, you can conclude that Horatio Alger's novels are about

    (a) poor people
    (b) rich people getting richer
    (c) poor people getting rich
    (d) rich people

8. Look at the block of letters below. Inside the block, there are some people's names from the passage. How many can you find? The names can go in any direction.

```
A  R  B  O  L  E  Y  A  Z

L  Z  K  N  M  L  Q  S  T

G  A  L  B  R  E  A  T  H

E  D  X  T  R  E  U  S  D

R  A  O  E  C  F  A  N  G

P  L  M  O  R  T  O  N  V
```

Check your answers on page 98.

9. **(For discussion)** Many people think of success as making a lot of money. But the successful people in the passage all talked about something else. They talked about challenges, and about meeting those challenges. They talked about achieving goals. This is how many people who have "made it" think of success. What are some of your goals? If you achieved those goals, would you feel success-ful? Would you set new, higher goals for yourself, or would you be happy with what you had?

I am not a computer expert. I have been in the field for only a short time. I never learned much in the way of science or math. And I am quite puzzled by things like engineering or electronics.

Then why am I able to write about computers? I can write on this subject *because* of these shortcomings. The last two years of learning have been an ordeal for me. By hard work I have managed to learn enough to use computers fairly well, and to work with people who know a great deal more than I. Since I have learned all this at such personal cost, I would like to share my knowledge with others. More and more people want to know about computers, and want to know quickly.

The best way to learn is to take a course. However, many people do not have the time for this. They will have to find some other way to get some basic information. I hope to be able to help them by writing about some of the things I have learned myself.

I have a home computer on which I've learned in my own time. I have used it like a home study course. I have sat down with it day after day, night after night. I have forced it to give up some of its secrets. Now I can use it to do some of the work that I get paid for. And I can do this work in my own home, instead of in an office. Many people may soon be working on a computer at home, just as many now take in other people's typing.

Some things about computers are easier than you may fear. First, computers are logical. Things that at first seem difficult will make sense to you after you learn the rules. Second, it is really not hard to learn enough to use today's machines. You do not need to be a great brain. But you do have to learn to think in new ways. And you do have to keep a good bit of information in your head. Finally, there are many people around who are really enthusiastic about computers. These people are always happy to be of help. □

Adapted from *Understanding Microcomputers* by Rose Deakin. New York: New American Library, 1983. Pp. 11–14, 44–45.

1. The purpose of the passage is to convince readers that, by studying computers at home, people can become

   (a) computer experts
   (b) writers about computers
   (c) computer programmers
   (d) skilled amateurs

2. According to the passage, all of the following statements about the author are true EXCEPT:

   (a) She knows more than her co-workers.
   (b) She knows very little science or math.
   (c) She knows many things about computers.
   (d) She can help others with computers.

3. According to the passage, a home computer can best be described as

   (a) puzzling   (c) logical
   (b) secret   (d) difficult

4. From the passage, you can conclude that in order to write about computers, the author had to

   (a) study very hard
   (b) take a home study course
   (c) learn electronics
   (d) learn from other people

5. The author believes that one of the most useful things about many people who understand computers is that they are

   (a) all logical
   (b) eager to help
   (c) teaching computer courses
   (d) engineers and scientists

6. You can conclude that the author thinks that if a person took a computer course, that person would learn

   (a) very quickly
   (b) as much as the author's co-workers
   (c) to think like a computer
   (d) about computers the easy way

7. According to the passage, a computer can be used at home to help you

   (a) study school work
   (b) take in typing
   (c) change your home into an office
   (d) earn some money

8. The author uses the word "ordeal" in the second paragraph to mean something that is

   (a) difficult   **(c)** frightening
   (b) boring   **(d)** short

9. There are <u>3</u> four-letter words hidden in the words **HOME COMPUTER.** Use the clues for help. Use each letter only ONCE!

    (a) C _ _ _   (someone's pal)
    (b) P _ _ _   (a verse)
    (c) T _ _ _   (ripped)

Check your answers on page 99.

9

More and more people are finding out what a group can do. They're finding that a group can do much more than a person acting alone. Today, home owners form groups to improve their neighborhoods. Tenants unite to deal with their landlords. Shoppers can join co-ops to buy food and other items at group rates. They fight high prices by getting together and buying goods in large amounts. People also form groups to help hospitals, schools, and senior citizens.

People form groups to help themselves. They join because of the things they will gain. The answer to the question, "What's in it for me?" is often why people take part in groups.

But everyone must do his or her part for any group to get things done. Members must take on responsibilities. Group action means that everyone does something. Some things to remember when you start or join a group are:

- **Attend meetings.** "I don't know what's going on," is a gripe often heard at meetings. Chances are the person hasn't been to a meeting in weeks.

- **Be on time.** Members who are always late disturb other members and slow down meetings.

- **Ask questions.** If you're confused at a meeting, probably others are, too. A quick answer will make things easier for everyone.

- **Speak up.** Many times, a few people who talk all the time run the show. They can only do this if the rest of the members are afraid to open their mouths.

- **Go by the vote.** You can always argue for or against something. And you can always vote. But if you lose, be a good sport and work with the group. The member who quits because he or she is out-voted loses for good.

- **Do your job.** If you say you'll do a job for the group, follow through. But don't let yourself be pressured to do something you don't have time for or think you can't handle. If you take on a task and your work or family situation changes, let the group know. They can get another member to pick up the job where you left off.

Together, people can get things done. They can protect their homes and improve their neighborhoods. They can save themselves money and help others. Working in a group for common interests gives people the joy of doing things they couldn't do alone. There is strength in numbers. And as long as everyone does his or her part, the benefits can be great for all. □

Adapted from *Organizations, Clubs, Action Groups* by Elsie E. Wolfers and Virginia B. Evansen. New York: Penguin, 1982. Pp. ix, 1, 2.

1. The main idea of the passage is that people who join groups

   (a) are just thinking of themselves
   (b) need a place to go
   (c) should be active and responsible
   (d) get less done than people who act alone

2. According to the author, a person joins any group because he or she has found the answer to the question,

   (a) "What's in it for me?"
   (b) "How can I start a co-op?"
   (c) "What's the best way to deal with my landlord?"
   (d) "How can I help senior citizens?"

3. All of the following describe ways of being a responsible group member EXCEPT

   (a) ask questions
   (b) don't be late for meetings
   (c) do the job you promised to do
   (d) always be quiet, and don't talk at meetings

4. From the information in the passage, you can conclude that because people act together in a group all might want to

   (a) run the group
   (b) fight with each other
   (c) work as little as possible
   (d) help the community

5. Which of the following could best be used in place of the sentence "There is strength in numbers" in the last paragraph?

   (a) Strong people are always counted.
   (b) Money is power.
   (c) A group can do more than one person.
   (d) People can get what they want if they are strong.

6. The word "gripe," used in the fourth paragraph, most nearly means

   (a) dialogue   **(c)** saying
   (b) complaint   **(d)** speech

Check your answers on page 101.

7. **(For discussion)**   Since the beginning of history, people have formed groups. These groups have been formed for political reasons, religious reasons, and for other reasons that were important to the people who formed them. Think about some groups formed in the past. How were they formed? Why were they formed?
   The passage tells you about some of the responsibilities of group members today. But think about the groups of the past. Did members of those groups have the same kinds of responsibilities? Why or why not?

My work is trying to change this country. This is the job I've chosen. When people ask me, "Why are you doing this?" it's like asking what kind of sickness you've got. I don't feel sick. I think this country is sick. The daily injustices just gnaw on me a little harder than they do on other people.

I try to bring people together who are being put down by the system, left out. You try to build an organization that will give them power to make the changes. Everybody's at the bottom of the barrel at this point. Ten years ago one could say the poor people suffered and the middle class got by. That's not true anymore.

I came to East Kentucky with the OEO (Office of Economic Opportunity). I got canned in a year. Their idea was to support the right candidates. I didn't see that as my work. My job was to build an organization of put-down people.

I put together a fairly solid organization of Appalachian people in Pike County. It's a single industry area: coal. You either work for the coal company or you don't work. Sixty percent of its people live on incomes lower than the government's guidelines for rural areas.

So what I'm saying is, it's possible to win, to take an outfit like Bethlehem Steel and lick 'em. Most people in their guts don't really believe it. Gee, it's great when all of a sudden they realize it's possible. They become alive.

Nobody believed PCCA (Pike County Citizens Association) could stop Bethlehem from strip mining. Ten miles away was a hillside being stripped. Ten miles is like ten million light years away. What they wanted was a park, a place for their kids. Bethlehem said, "Go to hell. You're just a bunch of crummy Appalachians. We're not gonna give you a damn thing." If I could get that park for them, they would believe it's possible to do other things.

They really needed a victory. They had lost over and over again, day after day. So I got together twenty, thirty people I saw as leaders. I said, "Let's get that park." They said, "We can't." I said, "We can. If we let all the big wheels around the country know—the National Council of Churches and everybody start calling up, writing, and hounding Bethlehem. They'll have to give us the park."

That's exactly what happened. Bethlehem thought: This is getting to be a pain. We'll give them the park and they'll shut up about strip mining. We haven't shut up on strip mining, but we got the park. Four thousand people from Pike County drove up and watched those bulldozers grading down that park. It was an incredible victory.

People become afraid of each other. They're convinced there's not a damn thing they can do. I think we have it inside us to change things. We need the courage. It's a scary thing. Because we've been told from the time we were born that what we have inside us is bad and useless. What's true is what we have inside us is good and useful. □

Condensed from "Bill Talcott," *Working* by Studs Terkel. New York: Pantheon Books, 1973.

1. The main purpose of the passage is to show that people

    (a) should fight Bethlehem Steel
    (b) should always fight big companies
    (c) have the power inside themselves to change things
    (d) have the power to take over steel companies

2. The author's opinion of the country is that it is

    (a) sick   **(c)** dangerous
    (b) fair   **(d)** loving

3. According to the author, most people don't fight back against big companies because they

    (a) don't have the time
    (b) don't have the energy
    (c) think the companies will win
    (d) think the companies are right

4. The author suggests that after the people of Pike County forced Bethlehem Steel to build a park, the people would

   (a) think of Bethlehem Steel as their friend
   (b) believe it's possible to do other things
   (c) thank Bethlehem Steel for building the park
   (d) not force Bethlehem Steel to stop strip mining

5. From the information in the passage, you can conclude that the people of Pike County can fight

   (a) any big company and still win
   (b) for their rights if they are organized
   (c) Bethlehem Steel again and still win
   (d) for their rights only if the author helps

6. From the information in the passage, what do you think the National Council of Churches probably did that helped the people of Pike County fight Bethlehem Steel?

   (a) called up big wheels around the country
   (b) collected money to buy the park land
   (c) put pressure on Bethlehem
   (d) paid the author's salary

7. The author believes that people can be useful and can change things, but first they must

   (a) gain a victory for their community
   (b) find a leader like the author of the passage
   (c) build a national organization
   (d) have the courage to believe they are good and useful

8. In the last sentence in the third paragraph, the word "rural" means

   (a) city   (c) desert
   (b) seashore   (d) country

9. Solve this puzzle by using words from the list:

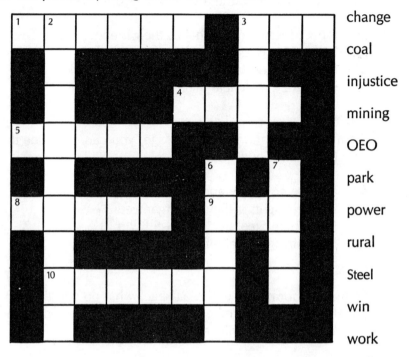

change

coal

injustice

mining

OEO

park

power

rural

Steel

win

work

Across

1. The people of Pike County wanted to stop Bethlehem from strip _____.
3. The author says it's possible for people working together to _____.
4 The group's first success was in getting a _____.
5. From the fourth paragraph you can infer that Pike County is a _____ area.
8. The major employer in Pike County is Bethlehem _____.
9. The author's first job in East Kentucky was with the _____.

10. The author is trying to get people organized so they can _____ things they don't like.

Down

2. In the first paragraph the author says he feels _____ more strongly than most people.
3. He says his _____ is trying to change this country.
6. In the second paragraph he says that he tries to get people to organize so they can have more _____.
7. Most of the people in Pike County work for the _____ company.

Check your answers on page 102.

10. **(For discussion)**   There's an old saying, "You can't fight City
     Hall." It's a way of saying that "little people" shouldn't try to
     change things when a big company or the government does some-
     thing they don't like. Are there any problems in your area caused
     by "City Hall?" What are they? Now that you've read the passage,
     what are some ways you could start to change things? What
     would <u>you</u> do? What would you do <u>first</u>?

11

In March of 1962, the black people of Selma, Alabama, first
tried to march to the state capital at Montgomery. They
marched to demand their right to vote. Governor George
Wallace had ordered the march stopped. Sheriff Jim Clark and
a large posse on horseback were waiting for the marchers on
a bridge along the way. They turned back the march with
brutal force. Even though she was only eight years old at the
time, Sheyanne Webb was on the march. She remembers:

When I first got to the church that night, my eyes were still
swollen and burning from the tear gas. But what I saw there
made me cry again. I'll never forget the faces of those people.
I'd never seen such looks before. I remember standing and
looking at them a long time before sitting down. They weren't
afraid, because they were too beaten to know any more fear.
It was as though nobody cared to even try to win anything
anymore. It was as if we had been put in our place by a good
beating.

I sat up toward the front. Now there were a bunch of kids
up there. So we were just sitting there crying, listening to the
others cry. Some were even moaning and wailing. It was an
awful thing. It was like we were at our own funeral.

But then later in the night, maybe nine-thirty or ten, I don't
know for sure, all of a sudden somebody there started hum-

ming. I think they were moaning and it just went into the humming of a freedom song. It was real low, but some of us children began humming along, slow and soft. At first I didn't even know what it was, what song, I mean. It was like a funeral sound, a dirge. Then I recognized it—*Ain't Gonna Let Nobody Turn Me 'Round.* I'd never heard it or hummed it that way before. But it just started to catch on, and the people began to pick it up. It started to swell, the humming. Then we began singing the words. We sang, "Ain't gonna let George Wallace turn me 'round." And, "Ain't gonna let Jim Clark turn me 'round." "Ain't gonna let no state trooper turn me 'round."

Ain't gonna let no horses . . . ain't gonna let no tear gas— ain't gonna let nobody turn me 'round. *Nobody!*

And everybody's singing now, and some of them are clapping their hands. They're still crying, but it's a different kind of crying. It's the kind of crying that's got spirit, not the weeping they had been doing.

We were singing and telling the world that we hadn't been whipped, that we had won.

Just all of a sudden something happened that night and we knew in that church that—Lord Almighty—we had really won, after all. We had won!

And Reverend Reese was up at the pulpit, and he announced that Dr. King called. Dr. King said he was coming back the next day and he was bringing help for us. Well, it was that night that the whole nation—even the whole world—saw what had happened that day in Selma. The television cameras had gotten the whole thing.

When I first went into that church that evening those people sitting there were beaten. I mean their spirit, their will was beaten. But when that singing started, we grew stronger. Each one of us said to ourselves that we could go back out there. We could face the tear gas, face the horses. We could face whatever Jim Clark could throw at us.

Reverend Reese said later that what happened at the church that night was the turning point in the voting-rights drive in Selma. Our nonviolent approach had been threatened, because so many people were angry and wanted to get even with the possemen and the troopers. If that had happened, our efforts to point out the injustice in Alabama might have been lost. If our people had allowed themselves to become common rioters, the sympathy we gained from the days and days of marching would have been for nothing. After the beating at the bridge, we faced a crisis point in our movement. Despite what we had gone through at the bridge and in the streets, we had to hold on to our sense of dignity. We had to keep it. □

Condensed from "Sheyanne Webb," Chapter 19, from *Selma, Lord, Selma* by Sheyanne Webb, Rachel Nelson West and Frank Sikora. University of Alabama Press, 1980.

1. According to the passage, the black people of Selma tried to march to the state capitol to demand

    (a) peace in Selma   (c) black women's rights
    (b) their right to vote   (d) a new governor

2. The word "wailing" as it is used in the third paragraph most nearly means

    (a) singing out loud   (c) weeping out loud
    (b) speaking out loud   (d) praying out loud

3. The author suggests that when the people in the church began to sing, they felt

    (a) strong   (c) depressed
    (b) free   (d) afraid

4. The word "dirge" most nearly means a

    (a) sharp cry   (c) sad song
    (b) soft prayer   (d) strong speech

5. According to the passage, the whole nation knew what had happened at Selma because

   (a) the author told her story
   (b) it was on television
   (c) the governor made a speech
   (d) so many people were hurt

6. When the author arrived at the church, she says she started to cry because the people

   (a) had lost their fear
   (b) looked beaten and defeated
   (c) were crying
   (d) had been tear gassed

7. The Reverend Reese says that a turning point in the voting-rights drive was reached on the night Sheyanne describes. What do you think happened that night in Selma that makes this true?

   (a) The people wanted to fight.
   (b) The people kept their dignity.
   (c) Everyone sang together.
   (d) Everyone got the vote.

8. According to the passage, Dr. King came back to Selma before the people

   (a) started to march
   (b) were seen on television
   (c) were stopped by the police
   (d) got their right to vote

Check your answers on page 104.

9. **(For discussion)** When the author says, "We had really won, after all. We had won!", what do you think she means? What did the people on the Selma march win?

10. **(For discussion)** Sheyanne Webb says that the whole world had seen the brutal force of the police on TV. People saw that the marchers were peaceful and that the police were the ones who were violent. This sight made people all over the country—and the world—angry. Millions of people began to support the voting-rights movement in the South. This sight changed public opinion. And TV is what did it. Can you think of other examples of TV changing public opinion? How did it happen? Why?

Electricity is a form of energy. It exists in nature, where you can sometimes see it in the form of lightning. Lightning can be destructive. You may also feel it in the harmless form of static electricity. This is the spark that goes off when you touch something after you have walked on a thick carpet. You may also feel static electricity when you brush your hair.

You cannot see electricity. It has no color, size, or weight. Yet people have learned how to make it and deliver it in a split second.

Your electric company does this from the energy found in natural fuels. The energy stored in oil, uranium, and natural gas is converted into electricity. Electricity can also be made from the energy in coal and falling water. Other possible sources are the winds, tides, sunlight, and the heat contained in the earth. However, these sources do not yet produce energy in the quantities people need, or at prices as low as those of the more usual fuels.

To make electricity, your electric company uses the natural fuels to boil vast amounts of water. This produces steam, which is used to turn turbine generators. The turbine generators are where the electricity is made. They create, or generate, a flow of current.

The current flows from the generator through cables. These cables lead from the generating plant to a substation. (See illustration.) They carry a great deal of electric current. The high-voltage cables have to be kept several feet apart from one another. These overhead wires are supported by poles at regular distances. A material through which electricity cannot pass is used where the wires meet the poles. These insulators keep the electricity from traveling through the poles to the ground.

Any time an insulator is broken, it is possible that the wire or pole might fall to the ground. This creates the danger of electric shock for anyone who might come in contact with it. If you see a wire or pole that is down, do not touch or go near it. Keep other people away, too. Notify your electric company and the police. Do not touch anything that may be touching a downed power line. Stay away from any place where signs warn, "Danger, High Voltage." The signs are placed there to protect your life, not to protect the equipment.

At substations, power is reduced to lower voltages. Then it is sent out for use in your home. Before it enters your home, the electricity is put through a transformer. The transformer makes the voltage even lower. This is necessary because the wires in your house could not handle the voltage that comes from the substation. They are too small and would burn up. When it enters your home, the electricity goes through a meter placed there by the electric company. The meter measures the

How Electricity Gets Into Your Home

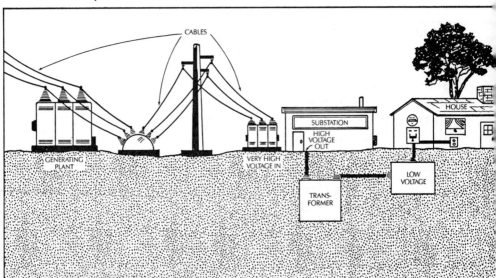

amount of electricity you use. Inside your home, the current flows through wires inside the walls to the wall sockets.

The network that brings electricity to your home is designed to do this in the safest way possible. From there on, the use of electricity is in your hands. Use it safely, because care will prevent accidents. ☐

Adapted from "How Electricity is Made," *Using Electricity Safely*, Con Edison, 1977.

1. Which of the following would be the best title for the passage?

    (a) Safety with Electricity
    (b) Electricity: From Nature to You
    (c) The Uses of Electrical Energy
    (d) Electrical Generators at Work

2. As it is used in the passage, the word "insulator" means something that

    (a) breaks easily   **(c)** carries electricity
    (b) can't be broken   **(d)** doesn't carry electricity

3. According to the passage, which of the following statements about electricity is true?

    (a) It is always very hot.
    (b) It passes through insulators.
    (c) It produces huge amounts of steam.
    (d) It is colorless and weightless.

4. From the passage you can conclude that producing electricity depends mainly on

    (a) heat stored in the earth
    (b) the energy of natural fuels
    (c) creating a magnetic field
    (d) winds, tides, and sunlight

5. According to the passage and the drawing on page 36, the over-head cables running from a generating plant to a substation are carrying

   (a) electricity for your home
   (b) high-voltage electricity
   (c) electricity to a transformer
   (d) low-voltage electricity

6. According to the information in the passage, you can infer that the author tells you not to touch something that's in contact with a downed power line because

   (a) another power line may fall
   (b) the wire may be broken
   (c) there may be no insulation
   (d) a support pole may fall

7. According to the passage, you can conclude that power from generators cannot enter your home until

   (a) the voltage is lowered
   (b) a meter is turned on
   (c) overhead wires are built
   (d) equipment is protected

8. Which of the following words is closest to the meaning of the word "converted" used in the third paragraph?

   (a) united   (c) transmitted
   (b) generated   (d) changed

Check your answers on page 106.

~~~~~~~~ *13* ~~~~~~

Perhaps the kids came home from school with cramps, diarrhea, vomiting, fever. Or perhaps you missed a few days work because of the same symptoms. In either case, you may say that it was just "a bug that was going around." But the bug you caught—or that caught you—may well have been food poisoning. And you may have sent the "bug" to school or work in the brown bag lunch you packed.

A few simple methods are the key to packing a safe brown bag lunch. The precautions may save you and your family a lot of grief.

First, cook food thoroughly. If it's meant to be hot, keep it hot. If it's meant to be cool, keep it cool. Bacteria thrive between 45°F and 115°F. Cool foods should be below 45°F, and hot foods over 115°F.

A thermos bottle is a good way to keep hot foods hot and cold foods cold. There are other ways to keep foods cold as well. The best is to keep your bag lunch in a refrigerator at school or at work. That is not always possible, though.

A freezer gel pack can be put into the bag next to your sandwich. Buy one at the housewares counter and keep it in the freezer overnight. Or you can make your own freezer pack by taking a small plastic container with a secure lid. Fill it nearly to the top with water and place in freezer. Wrap it in a plastic bag before using.

Another method is to freeze your chicken or meat sandwich. It will thaw in time for lunch, and help keep the rest of your food cold until then. Never let your lunch bag sit on top of a radiator or other warm place. This helps bacteria to grow.

Hot foods should be boiling hot when poured into a thermos bottle. All vegetables and fruits should be clean and well scrubbed.

Keep everything used to prepare lunches clean. Wash counter tops thoroughly with soap and hot water. The same goes for your hands. If you have cuts or sores, wear rubber gloves when preparing food. Wash thermos bottles and rinse with boiling water after use. Use a fork, not your fingers, to place meat or cheese in the sandwich. Fingers can spread bacteria.

It's a good idea to use a lunch box instead of a paper bag. And it's easy to keep a box clean.

How can you tell if you get food poisoning? Sometimes you can't. The "bug" the kids came home with might have been something else. But if you get a severe headache, diarrhea, vomiting, stomach cramps, and a fever soon after eating, there's a good chance it's food poisoning. Because the symptoms are similar, flu and food poisoning are often mistaken for each other. Food poisoning is rarely fatal. But it can be. And it affects infants and elderly people more severely.

The important thing to remember is—don't take chances. You can prevent food poisoning easily enough. ☐

Adapted from *Safe Brown Bag Lunches,* a pamphlet from the Food Safety and Quality Service, U.S. Department of Agriculture, 1977.

1. Which of the following would be the best title for the passage?

   (a) Making Good Lunches
   (b) Food Poisoning and the Flu
   (c) How to Prevent Food Poisoning
   (d) Symptoms of Food Poisoning

2. All of the following are things to remember when making brown bag lunches EXCEPT:

   (a) Cook all food thoroughly.
   (b) Keep everything used to prepare lunches clean.
   (c) Use a thermos to keep foods hot or cold.
   (d) Never freeze chicken or meat sandwiches.

3. According to the passage, if you prepare a safe bag lunch, the person who eats it will not get

   (a) a "bug"   (c) food poisoning
   (b) hungry   (d) the flu

4. With which of the following statements about preparing food would the author of the passage probably agree?

   (a) Being careful can help you stay healthy.
   (b) It's hard to prepare safe bag lunches.
   (c) Everyone will get food poisoning at least once.
   (d) Food poisoning and flu are caused by the same "bug."

5. The word "precautions" in the second paragraph most nearly means

   (a) warning signs   (c) safety measures
   (b) danger signals   (d) cooking methods

6. How many ways of preparing food mentioned in this passage can you find? Circle each word you find. Words can be read across or up and down.

```
F  S  G  K  S  E
D  C  L  H  J  R
F  R  E  E  Z  E
W  U  C  L  Q  R
A  B  O  I  L  S
S  L  O  M  F  G
H  Z  K  E  N  Z
```

7. The word "symptom" most nearly means

   (a) sign   (c) illness
   (b) disease   (d) cause

8. From the information in the passage, you can infer that if you have cuts or sores, you should wear rubber gloves when preparing food because

    (a) gloves will protect you from infection
    (b) cuts and sores may contain bacteria
    (c) gloves are easier to keep clean than your hands
    (d) a cut or sore may hurt when you wash your hands

Check your answers on page 108.

~~~~~~~~~ **14** ~~~~~~

In the past, almost everything written about having a baby was addressed to women. Everyone focused on the mother-to-be and the baby growing inside her body. Many men felt useless. They felt they were needed about as much as an extra leg.

Ah, but now things—and thinking—are changing! Studies have found that men *are* important to the growing of a whole new human being.

Of course, a child can develop into a worthwhile person without the presence of a father. There have been many people who never knew their fathers and still became useful and remarkable adults.

Still, good fathering is just as important to human offspring as good mothering. It isn't just that the extra pair of hands is always welcome! A man's presence makes so much more possible for a child. A father is not just a "mother's helper." He is a parent who is fathering.

Of course, no man should try to fit into a mold which makes him uncomfortable. In my grandfather's day, most men worked very long hours. They hardly ever saw their children awake. My father never bathed a baby or gave much daily care. But he did spend his little spare time with his babies, and a lot more with his grandchildren. My children's father, on the other hand, played with and fed his babies. He bathed them. He learned a lot about them.

Today the men of my son's and daughter's age often share in the experience of having a baby. Men are preparing for fatherhood. They are in the prenatal classes with the mother-to-be. They're often in the labor room. They may even be present during the birth. And they often share the details of daily care after the baby arrives.

This sharing may come easily to many fathers. But it may be harder for others. However, men do have free choice. Some may choose to be less involved preparing for birth. Everything is not for everyone! You can stay out of the delivery room without feeling like a traitor to the mother or baby. You can be a great father, and never bathe or dress your infant.

Fathering comes in many styles. Its one essential ingredient is loving. But loving doesn't mean doing everything. Loving means giving to, and giving up, for someone else's welfare.

Here are some ways to prepare for being a father:

- Think about fatherhood. Be excited about it. Enjoy the idea of becoming a *family!*

- Talk with and listen to your baby's mother. Share your worries with her. Urge her to share her worries with you.

- Go the library for books and magazines about having a baby. Learn about pregnancy, and about how babies grow.

- Talk to other men about fathering. You can learn a great deal about babies from other parents. Be sure to ask the fathers you know about the pleasure they get from their children!

- And after your baby arrives, talk to other men about *your* experiences. The joys of fathering will grow, and the problems will shrink, when you share them with other men. □

Adapted from *Preparing for Your New Baby* by Shirley Camper Soman. New York: Delacorte Press, 1982. Pp. 27, 28.

1. The main idea of the passage is that men should spend time with their children because

    (a) children love to play with their fathers
    (b) mothers don't always have time to do everything
    (c) children need fathers as much as mothers
    (d) mothers expect fathers to fit a mold

2. All of the following are ways to prepare for being a father EXCEPT:

    (a) bathing and dressing infants
    (b) talking to other men
    (c) talking about fatherhood
    (d) reading books and magazines

3. According to the passage, if a new father shares his experiences with other fathers, his

    (a) friends will respect him
    (b) baby will be happier
    (c) fears will shrink
    (d) joys will grow

4. According to the passage, fathers spent less time with their children years ago than they do today because they

    (a) had to work longer hours
    (b) were not interested in fathering
    (c) didn't love their families
    (d) were uncomfortable being fathers

5. The author seems to believe that the most important part of fathering is

    (a) sharing the daily care of the baby
    (b) being present in the labor room
    (c) bathing and dressing the infant
    (d) giving to and giving up for someone else

6. According to the author, men today often share in all of the following EXCEPT

    (a) attending classes with the mother-to-be
    (b) helping the doctor deliver the baby
    (c) caring for the new baby at home
    (d) staying in the labor room with the mother

7. The author's attitude toward fathers is best described as

    (a) worried   (c) encouraging
    (b) amused   (d) unfair

8. Which of the following is closest in meaning to the word "prenatal" in the sixth paragraph?

    (a) parent training   (c) childbirth
    (b) child care   (d) before birth

Check your answers on page 110.

9. **(For discussion)**   Think of the fathers you know. Are they helping with the care of their children? Describe an example of good fathering you have seen. Describe an example of bad fathering. What could that father have done instead?

15

Mary Volino worked for two years in a small company. She started out in the accounting department. Then she was transferred to purchasing.

I wasn't in purchasing but a month when I realized that I was pregnant. I had a male boss. But I went immediately to my old boss, Joan. I told her I was pregnant and she said, "Wow, that's fantastic." I said I didn't know if I would have the baby. I wasn't sure what I wanted at that point. And she said, "Well, listen, don't worry about it." I told her I would like a job to come back to if I decided to have the baby. "Don't worry about anything like that," she said. "Except in your seventh month, I don't think it would be a good idea if you stuck around because you'll be too big." So at that point I figured, well, yeah, that sounds logical to me. Besides, I'd like some time for myself. It'll give me a few months before I have the baby, and then I'll go back to work. So I tripped along on my merry little way.

I didn't get along with my boss, Don. He became unglued when I started to wear maternity clothes. He would scream and start picking on me. Women frightened him. So here I am getting bigger and bigger and it's time for my raise. He keeps putting me off. He tells me, "Well, since you're leaving, there's no reason for you to get a raise." And I say, "But I've worked all this time without a raise. I'm due for a raise right now." And he says, "No, I'm working out something good for you. You can get it all in one lump sum when you leave." We go back and forth. He says that Joan is the one that's holding my raise back, and she says it's him.

So he starts in about my seventh month. I'm just realizing that I can't give up this job so easily. I really need the money. He keeps saying to me, "Well, when are you going to leave?" I keep saying in a couple of weeks. We're going back and forth like this. God knows why. Some people said the front office didn't think it looked good to have me so big. I was the first woman ever to get pregnant there and they didn't know how to handle it. A few girls after me have gotten pregnant, and they've let all of them go, too.

So I'm just assuming it's OK, you know. State law says that you cannot be let go because of pregnancy. There has to be a job waiting for you after six weeks. Don told me that he couldn't keep the job in purchasing open, and I said, "Yes, I understood that." But he said, "There's got to be something else. You can pitch in somewhere." And it was an understood fact from the very beginning. I mean, I never went back to Joan and made sure, definitely. But she had said it in the beginning. Why should I think anything else?

Anyway, the day that I was leaving they had this form. I filled it out and brought it in to Joan. And where it says,

"Remarks," I had put down "Nine months maternity leave." She took it and scratched it out. She said, "We don't have anything like maternity leave. If you want a job, you're going to have to come in and fill out an application." Just like any other slob on the street.

Well, I was crushed. I mean I was really crushed. When she said that about coming in and filling out an application, I just looked at her. Because I loved that job. I mean, it was the first job that I ever felt capable and confident in. So I just got up and walked out of there, defeated. I didn't know how to deal with it. I was trying to keep myself together. A brave front. Walking out with my head held high.

They bought me off with a $200 baby gift. A check. *And* they took taxes out of it.

Then I had a big legal battle at unemployment. At first I waited a month before going. I bought Joan's stuff hook, line and sinker: "You quit and that's it." She sold me a bill of goods and I bought it. But my husband kept saying, "Go, go, it's legal." So I finally went. Unemployment didn't know how to handle my case because there was nothing written down except the thing about maternity leave that Joan scratched out. I explained it to the guy and he couldn't believe what was happening. He said, "Wow, I don't know, I've got to talk to my supervisor." The supervisor called me and kept asking me over and over again the facts. What was said back and forth. Plus Joan was giving him the runaround. First she wouldn't answer the phone. And the company kept writing on the papers, "Quit because of pregnancy."

I finally said, "Listen, talk to Don. Maybe he'll help me." And I called him up. He knew what financial position my husband and me were in. And I said, "Don, you've got to make them give it to me. You can't say that I quit. Get that paper where I requested maternity leave." And he said, "All right, don't worry. I'll take care of it." I don't know what he did, but I got the unemployment.

And I decided to run it to the hilt. Just run it, man, to the bloody end. And I did. Seventeen months of unemployment. I understood that their interest rates go up, and I just wanted to blow them right out of the world. Screw them like they screwed me. □

Adapted from "Mary Volino," *Not Working* by Harry Maurer. New York: Holt, Rinehart & Winston 1979.

1. The best title for this passage would be

   (a) Applying For Maternity Leave
   (b) Applying for Unemployment Benefits
   (c) Working Mothers and Their Jobs
   (d) A Working Woman Demands Her Rights

2. The author thought she would keep her job because

   (a) her old boss told her not to worry
   (b) she had just started in a new department
   (c) other girls in the office were pregnant
   (d) she needed the money for her baby

3. When the author left her job, she received

   (a) more than $200
   (b) less than $200
   (c) state aid for mothers
   (d) a job application

4. According to the passage, when the author knew she was pregnant, she told her boss first because

   (a) she wanted maternity leave
   (b) she didn't like her new job
   (c) her old boss was a woman
   (d) her new boss didn't like her

5. According to the passage, the author did not want to leave her job when she was seven months pregnant because she

   (a) liked her job
   (b) couldn't afford to
   (c) didn't want to stay at home
   (d) liked her boss

6. From the information in the passage, you can conclude that the author waited a month before going to the unemployment office because she

    (a) was having her first baby
    (b) did not need the money
    (c) was ashamed because she had been fired
    (d) thought she couldn't get unemployment benefits

7. From the information in the passage, you can infer that the author was not the only woman with this problem because

    (a) other pregnant women had also lost their jobs
    (b) other mothers were at the unemployment office
    (c) her husband said it's legal to fire pregnant women
    (d) the unemployment supervisor told her about others

Check your answers on page 111.

8. **(For discussion)** Suppose you were in the author's situation. What would you have told your supervisor? What would you have done differently? Do you think employers should provide maternity leaves for their workers? Why or why not?

〰〰〰〰 *16* 〰〰〰〰〰〰〰〰〰〰〰〰〰〰〰〰〰〰〰〰〰〰〰

I came up here four years ago. I hadn't finished high school. Just seventeen years old. I knew I had to get a job, so I went to work for a big lumber company. Told them I was a maintenance man. I didn't know nothing about anything. They had all this machinery and construction stuff. I told them I knew how to take care of it. I didn't know how to do that. But hell, I knew I had to learn how to do something. So they hired me. And all the time I was there, see, I just watched this welder. I knew welders made good money and so I watched him work.

I'd say, "Hey, man, how do you do that?" and he'd show me. And I'd say, "Let me try," and he'd show me how to do it.

Hell, I wasn't doing no maintenance, not very much. I was watching that welder all the time. And he let me weld more and more, and hell, I learned how to weld. And as soon as I learned how to weld good enough, I quit that job. I went to work for another place. They asked me what I could do, and I said I was a welder.

"How do we know you're a welder?"

"I don't know if I can weld as good as you city dudes, but I can weld! Had my own truck back in West Virginia."

So they said, "Hell, come on. We'll give you a try."

Well, I wasn't the best welder then, but I learned how to be a pretty good welder. Made some mistakes at first, but I wasn't there but four or five months, and I was welding like crazy. But I realized there wasn't a helluva lot of money to be made there as a welder, so I said I'd go to work for a steel company and really make me some money. So I left that place and went to work for a steel company.

I get paid seven dollars and two cents an hour now, on federal jobs. And we do mostly federal jobs. Seven oh two an hour! And they know I'm a good welder now. So I work for four or five months and save me up some money and go down to West Virginia. Then I come back and work some more, and they haven't fired me yet. They tell me, "We know that you can find another job; we'll keep you on as long as you do good work for us."

And I said, "Hell yes, I'll work for you as long as you don't give me a hard time." □

Condensed from *Hard Living on Clay Street* by Joseph T. Howell. New York: Doubleday/Anchor, 1973. Pp. 341–342.

1. The author's first job was as a "maintenance man," and the company owned construction machinery. As a maintenance man, the author was supposed to

   (a) guard the machinery   (c) repair the machinery
   (b) run the machinery   (d) weld the machinery

2. According to the passage, which of the following kinds of work would the author prefer to do for a living?

    (a) any job in West Virginia
    (b) a lumber company foreman
    (c) running construction equipment
    (d) any job that paid well

3. Which of the following best describes what happened when the author's welding skills improved?

    (a) He got a raise from the lumber company.
    (b) He got a new job in West Virginia.
    (c) He got a better paying job with another lumber company.
    (d) He got a better paying job with a steel company.

4. With which of the following statements about federal jobs would the author most likely agree?

    (a) They are the hardest jobs to do well.
    (b) They are the easiest to be fired from.
    (c) They are good because they pay well.
    (d) They are the largest because the government needs big buildings.

5. From the information in the passage, what can you conclude that the author's feelings about his work are?

    (a) He doesn't like his fellow workers.
    (b) He enjoys being a welder, but he's still looking for something else.
    (c) He wants to make good money, but he doesn't want to give up his whole life to get it.
    (d) He's a good worker, and he would like to own his own welding truck.

6. When the author talks about his job experiences, his tone is

   (a) joking   **(c)** proud
   (b) sneaky   **(d)** bored

7. Which of the following would be the best title for this passage?

   (a) Working For a Steel Company
   (b) Getting Ahead on the Job
   (c) How to Become a Welder
   (d) Finding Your First Job

Check your answers on page 112.

8. **(For discussion)** To get two of his jobs the author had to lie about his experience. What would you have done in his place? Did he do the right thing? Can you think of any other way he could have gotten what he wanted without lying? Why do you think he chose to lie?

17

Hobart Foote is a utility man at the auto plant on the day shift. He has been there seventeen years. He is thirty-seven and looks older.

I like to work. Now two days this week have been kind of rough on me. I guess I come home grouchy. Absenteeism. When the men don't come to work, the utility men get stuck. One of us has got to cover his job until they bring a new man in there. Then we've got to show him the job.

We got this young generation in here. . . . They're not settled yet, and they just live from day to day. When they settle down, they do like myself. They get up and they have a routine. They go to work every day. I go to work here and if I didn't feel like going to work, I shoulda stayed home. But I feel if I go to work, I'll feel better after a while. And I do.

I think a lot of it is in your mind. You get like what's his name that works in the body shop. He's grown to hate the company. Not me. The company puts bread and butter on the table. I feed the family and with two teenaged kids, there's a lot of wants. And we're payin' for two cars. And I have brought home a forty-hour paycheck for Lord knows how long.

And that's why I work. And those other people when they settle down one of these days, they'll be what we call old-timers.

My day goes pretty good on the average. Used to it didn't, but now I have a pace. Who I joke with, who I tease about did they have to sleep in a car that night. Just something to keep your day going. I'm always jokin'.

It's the same routine. But I can rotate mine just a little bit, just enough to break the monotony. But when all of a sudden it's real quiet, nobody says nothing—that makes the day go real long. I'll look at the watch pin on my coveralls and see what time . . . it would be nine-twenty. And you look at your watch again and it's twenty-five minutes of ten. It seems like you worked forever. And it's been only roughly fifteen minutes. You want quittin' time so bad.

I'm proud of what my job gives me. Not the job. I couldn't say I'm proud of workin' for the Ford Motor Car Company. What makes it good is what the union and the company have negotiated over these period of years.

If a man's due any respect, he'll get respect. Got foremen in here I have no respect for whatsoever. Everyone is passing the buck. Management and they've got groups under them, and it spreads out just like a tree. Some foremen are trying to make it big, want to go to the top, and they don't last too long.

Thirteen more years with the company, it'll be thirty and out. When I retire, I'm gonna have me a little garden. A place down South. Do a little fishin', huntin'. Sit back, watch the sun come up, the sun go down. Keep my mind occupied. □

Condensed from "Hobart Foote," *Working* by Studs Terkel. New York: Pantheon Books, 1973.

1. Which of the following best states the author's opinion of his job?

    (a) It's rough because of the young generation.
    (b) It's boring and each day is long.
    (c) It's great because of the union.
    (d) It isn't the best, but I pay my bills.

2. According to the author, the young generation can best be described as

    (a) reliable   (c) routine
    (b) unsettled   (d) proud

3. In the passage, the author was grouchy because

    (a) some men didn't come to work
    (b) the job was too boring
    (c) he had too many bills to pay
    (d) he didn't respect the foreman

4. The author suggests that when the younger workers settle down they will

    (a) get the respect that is due to them
    (b) want to go to the top
    (c) go to work every day
    (d) grow to like the company

5. From the passage you can conclude that the author has been

    (a) laid off from time to time
    (b) working regularly
    (c) promoted to foreman
    (d) sick a great deal

6. From the passage, you can infer that most of the time, as far as his job goes, the author

   (a) is basically happy
   (b) has no friends
   (c) worries a lot
   (d) wants to quit

7. The author seems to think that the way you do your job can be most influenced by your

   (a) family   (c) expenses
   (b) management   (d) attitude

8. In the passage the author seems to think that his retirement is likely to be

   (a) lonely   (c) boring
   (b) difficult   (d) peaceful

9. Which of the following best expresses the meaning of "negoti-ated" in the seventh paragraph?

   (a) agreed on   (c) given out
   (b) built up   (d) argued over

Check your answers on page 114.

10. **(For discussion)** Can you think of some jobs that people look forward to, day after day? What are some things that can make a job bearable? What can make you hate your job? Is there anything you could do to change the way jobs affect working people?

18

One of the first things that I found when I first began being involved with some of the women's rights groups was that they acted like *their* attitude about housework was the only meaning housework could have. It was something they had to get their heads together on. I remember that our group, the Household Technicians of America, was doing a party for the feminist leader Gloria Steinem. It was over on the west side.

We were paid quite well, a professional fee, to work at that party. We had on black uniforms. It freaked out some of the feminist women there. They could not deal with it. They said, "Poor maids—they got maids here, we're leaving."

I remember having to stand up and say to them, "Hold it, cool it! First of all, I don't like you to think we're *maids*. We are household technicians. We're experienced, we're professionals. And we're being paid—that's very important. We need money. We're being paid, and we're going to be respected. So you have to get it out of your head that this is a dirty job. If you don't want to do it, I'm glad that you don't want to. Because we will gladly do it for you—but for a salary, and with respect. We want the same respect as other people get for a job, for a profession."

Most of my efforts have been getting that into other people's heads. And I explained to them that the uniform is the uniform of my profession. It's like a doctor wearing his white coat. I think you feel kind of uncomfortable if you go into his office and the doctor doesn't have his white coat on. You don't think of him as being a doctor. It's just the simple thing of a uniform, but it's there. And I said, "So I choose to wear my uniform. I'm not gonna ruin my clothes. You might spill something on me."

There was a good reaction. I think what my speech did was take away people's guilt feeling, that, "Oh, gee, now I don't have to feel guilty. She feels okay about it, so now I don't have to feel guilty." I think that's what it was. □

Adapted from *A Stranger in the House* by Robert Hamburger. New York: Macmillan, 1978. Pp. 163–164.

1. When the author says that women's rights groups had to "get their heads together" about housework, she means they had to

   (a) change their attitudes about what housework means
   (b) listen to the opinions of household workers
   (c) think more about the rights of household workers
   (d) let household workers join their organizations

2. Which of the following is the reason the author thinks of herself and the other household workers as professionals?

   (a) They are respected.
   (b) They belong to a group with a name.
   (c) They are experienced.
   (d) They are doing a dirty job.

3. From the information in the passage, you can conclude that the main thing the household workers took pride in was

   (a) the author's speed   (c) the money they earn
   (b) the work they do   (d) the group's attitude

4. At first, the guests wanted to leave the party because of the household workers. What were the workers doing that made the guests want to leave?

   (a) charging a large fee   (c) forming a group
   (b) spilling things   (d) doing housework

5. The "feminist" women at the party were most concerned with

   (a) Gloria Steinem's party
   (b) household workers' rights
   (c) the meaning of housework
   (d) women's rights

6. According to the passage, what is the main reason the author wore a uniform?

    (a) She felt like a doctor in the uniform.
    (b) The uniform let people know who she was.
    (c) Uniforms are less expensive than other clothes.
    (d) People at other parties had ruined her clothes.

Check your answers on page 116.

7. **(For discussion)** The author says that people have to stop thinking of housework as a "dirty job." People usually think this about jobs they don't want to do themselves. For many years, housework has been a job like this. What are some other "dirty jobs" that somebody has to do? What makes them seem unpleasant to many people? Do you think people like thinking that some jobs are "dirty?" Why or why not?

∞∞∞∞∞ *19* ∞∞∞∞∞∞∞∞∞∞∞∞∞∞∞∞∞∞∞∞∞∞∞∞∞∞∞∞∞∞∞∞∞∞∞∞

I've been working at the dealership for about eight or nine months, and I really like it. It's full time, actually it's more than full time. They don't pay me a lot of overtime, but I am learning a lot of specific stuff about Volvos. And I'm becoming a lot more efficient in my work. It's a four-year apprenticeship, and I have to go to school two nights a week all during those four years. And that's really a drag. I'm back at the junior college that I went to years ago, when I was just learning about cars.

The tables are really turned. Like, I know a whole lot more than some of the men that are there. Before, I was just, y'know, a freak. I guess I'm still a freak, 'cause there aren't any other women in the night program that I know of. But I have a little more credibility because I'm an apprentice at a dealership, and some of the guys are just working in gas stations. They're trying to, y'know, get to where I've finally gotten. But it's a drag. I'm not learning anything. School's a waste of my time, and I really resent having to be there two nights a week. I'd lose my job if I didn't go to the apprentice school, though.

The union has some deal worked out with the school about money. It's part of the conditions of my apprenticeship. If the union withdraws my apprenticeship, then I get fired from the job.

I also sort of resented being offered a four-year apprenticeship. I had asked for a two- or three-year one. I thought I would get some credit for my experience.

But I really didn't have any choice. Since it was the only apprenticeship I'd ever been offered, I wasn't going to refuse it because the terms were too long. But I think a man in my position could have bought a bunch of tools and rolled into a dealership or a big shop and convinced them he was working at journey level. Without any apprenticeship papers.

That's what I want to be able to do. That's why I want to finish this apprenticeship program. Because I just want to be able to go anywhere and work. I want to be able to rely on a skill. But I don't have any credibility without all those little pieces of paper.

My normal workday begins about six-thirty, quarter of seven. I get up and make coffee and make myself a lunch for the day and have breakfast. I have to be at work at eight.

I only live six blocks away from where I work, so I walk. I usually punch in at 7:59, slide in, and work takes off slowly the first hour or so. The day just sort of moves along.

There's a lot I could say about the people I work with and the various things that go on there. I really like all the people I work with. I think it's an amazing group of people that are somehow magically assembled there. I work with six or seven other mechanics, all men. They all help me and show me how to do jobs I don't know how to do. We do lubes, repairs, that sort of thing.

There's a woman at the parts counter. She's a first, too. She just got her journey level papers as a parts technician. She's neat, she just got married. I really like the people I work with, but I'm not sure I want to put energy out in their directions. I try to change the way they think sometimes, but it doesn't work. I mean, overall, most of these men see women as a class of subhumans. They make their individual exceptions, like me, for instance. That sort of scares me 'cause I don't know what makes me different. But I just don't try to change them like I used to. It doesn't get me anywhere. I expend all this energy and everything stays the same. □

Adapted from "Sandy Harold," *Blue Collar Women* by Mary Lindenstein Wolshok. New York: Doubleday/Anchor, 1981.

1. The best title for this passage would be

    (a) Prejudice Against Women
    (b) A Woman Takes a Man's Job Away
    (c) Women and the Unions
    (d) A Woman's Apprenticeship

2. In the second paragraph of the passage, the word "credibility" most nearly means able to be

    (a) honest   (c) believed
    (b) taught   (d) strong

3. From the information in the passage, you can infer that the author feels unhappy about going to college because

    (a) she would lose her job if she didn't go
    (b) the union has a deal worked out with the school
    (c) the school is not a famous college
    (d) she already knows the things the college is teaching

4. From the information in the passage, what can you conclude the author means when she says "everything stays the same," at the end of the passage?

    (a) The union can still tell her what to do and will not change.
    (b) She can't really change men's ideas about women.
    (c) A mechanic's job will never change.
    (d) She is afraid that the men she works with will never like her.

5. According to the passage, the author is working at a

   (a) dealership   (c) parts counter
   (b) gas station   (d) college

6. The author feels she needs to be in an apprenticeship program because she wants to

   (a) buy a bunch of tools
   (b) open a dealership
   (c) work anywhere she wants
   (d) learn a lot about Volvos

7. Why does the author resent being given a four-year apprenticeship?

   (a) She doesn't want to pay the college.
   (b) She thinks she should get credit for her experience.
   (c) She wants to work at journey level.
   (d) She wants to get another job.

8. What is the meaning of the word "journey" as it is used in the fifth and last paragraphs of the passage?

   (a) taking a trip
   (b) rank below apprenticeship
   (c) rank of parts technicians
   (d) rank above apprentice

Check your answers on page 118.

9. **(For discussion)** The author says she should get credit for her experience. How do you think she could prove she has experience?

10. **(For discussion)** Why do you think the author says that most of the men she works with see women as "a class of subhumans?" Why do you think the author says that she is an "exception?" What do you think she does differently?

20

Every afternoon when I came on duty as the evening nurse, I would walk the halls of the nursing home, pausing at each door to chat and observe. Often I would see Kate and Chris with their big scrapbooks on their laps. Proudly, Kate showed me pictures of bygone years. There was Chris, tall, blonde, handsome. And Kate, pretty, dark-haired, laughing. Two young lovers smiling through the passing seasons.

How lovely they looked now sitting there, the light shining on their white heads. Their time-wrinkled faces smiled at the memories of the years, caught and held forever in the scrapbooks.

How little the young know of loving, I would think. The old know what loving truly means. The young can only guess.

Kate and Chris were always together, always holding hands. As we staff members ate our evening meal, sometimes the two of them would pass by the dining-room doors. Then our talk would turn to them. We talked about their love, and what would happen when one of them died. We knew Chris was the strong one, and Kate was dependent on him. How would Kate manage if Chris died first, we often wondered.

Bedtime followed a ritual. Kate would be sitting in her chair, in nightgown and slippers. She was waiting for me to bring her medicine. Chris and I would watch while she took her pill. Then carefully he helped her from chair to bed and tucked the covers in around her frail body.

As I watched this act of love, I would think for the thousandth time, Good heavens, why don't nursing homes have double beds for married couples? All their lives they have slept together. But in a nursing home they're expected to sleep in single beds.

How foolish such policies are, I would think, as I watched Chris turn off the light above Kate's bed. Then he would bend over her and they would kiss gently. Chris would pat her cheek, and both would smile. He would pull up the side rail on her bed and only then would he turn and take his own medication. As I walked into the hall I could hear Chris say, "Goodnight, Kate." Her voice returned "Goodnight, Chris."

The space of an entire room separated their two beds.

I had been off duty two days. When I returned the first news I heard was that Chris had died the day before.

"How?"

"A heart attack. It happened quickly."

"How's Kate?"

"Bad."

I went into Kate's room. She was in her chair, motionless, staring.

"Kate, It's Phyllis. I just found out about Chris. I'm so sorry."

At the word "Chris," her eyes came back to life. Tears welled up and slid down her cheeks. "Chris is gone," she whispered.

"I know," I said. "I know."

We pampered Kate for a while. We let her eat in her room, and gave her special attention. Then gradually we worked her back into the daily schedule. Often, as I went past her room, I would see her in her chair. The scrapbooks were on her lap, and she gazed sadly at pictures of Chris.

Bedtime was the worst part of the day for Kate. She had been allowed to move from her bed to Chris's, as she had requested. The staff chatted and laughed with her as they tucked her in for the night. Yet Kate remained silent and sadly withdrawn. Passing her room an hour later I'd find her wide awake, staring at the ceiling.

The weeks passed and bedtime wasn't any better. One night I walked into her room, only to find the same wide-awake Kate. I said impulsively, "Kate, could it be you miss your goodnight kiss?" Bending down, I kissed her wrinkled cheek.

It was as though I had opened the floodgates. Tears streamed down her face. Her hands gripped mine. "Chris always kissed me goodnight," she cried.

"I know," I whispered.

"I miss him so much. All those years he kissed me good-night." She paused and I wiped her tears. "I just can't seem to go to sleep without his kiss."

She looked up at me, eyes brimming. "Oh, thank you for giving me a kiss." □

Adapted from "A Kiss for Kate" by Phyllis Volkens. *The Denver Post,* February 12, 1982.

1. Which of the following words could be used in place of "ritual" in the fifth paragraph?

    (a) different   **(c)** prayer
    (b) routine   **(d)** variety

2. All of the following titles could be used for this passage EXCEPT

    (a) The Goodnight Kiss
    (b) The Problem With Nursing Homes
    (c) A Love That Lasted
    (d) Old and Alone

3. After Chris tucked Kate into bed and turned off her light, he

    (a) read a book   **(c)** kissed her
    (b) put on pajamas   **(d)** talked to the author

4. The word "policies" in the seventh paragraph most nearly means

    (a) manners   **(c)** rules
    (b) ideas   **(d)** feelings

5. From the passage, you can conclude that the author thinks nursing homes should have double beds because

    (a) the beds are too far apart
    (b) Kate and Chris complained about their beds
    (c) double beds are more comfortable
    (d) married couples are used to sleeping together

6. From the information in the passage, you can infer that, after Chris died, bedtime was the hardest time for Kate because she

    (a) was afraid of the dark
    (b) couldn't sleep in a single bed
    (c) wanted more pills
    (d) felt most alone then

7. From the information in the passage, you can infer that the author kissed Kate goodnight because

    (a) Kate asked the author to
    (b) it would help Kate to sleep
    (c) it was part of the author's job
    (d) Kate was crying

8. According to the information in the passage, you can infer that the scrapbook held pictures of Chris and Kate

    (a) and their children
    (b) through their years together
    (c) in the nursing home
    (d) on their wedding day

9. Several words from the passage appear below. The words can be read across, down, or diagonally. Circle as many as you can find.

```
Z U E L F W T Y M W
F L O O D G A T E R
R I T U A L M D M I
A L E X J K N E O N
I R T O R O S E R K
L T I E L D P O I L
Q U P B Y G O N E T
P A M P E R T U S A
```

10. All of the following are true about Chris and Kate EXCEPT

   (a) they loved each other very much
   (b) they were both attractive when they were young
   (c) Chris was always lonely
   (d) Kate depended on Chris

Check your answers on page 120.

11. **(For discussion)**   In the third paragraph, the author says: "The old know what love truly means. The young can only guess." What do you think this statement means? Do you agree with this statement?

~~~~~~~~~ **21** ~~~~~~

What would you think, just offhand, is the most common street name in the United States? Pretend you win a hundred dollars if you guess right.

You'd have to say that, overall, we haven't shown a lot of originality with the names we've given our streets. In most countries the great streets have great-sounding names. London has half a dozen of them: Bond Street, Fleet Street, Carnaby Street, Piccadilly. What do we have? Michigan Avenue. Sunset Boulevard.

Some of our greatest streets don't even have names; they have numbers. In New York the classiest street in town is called Fifth Avenue. Some of the numbers in New York are even dull. Forty-second Street—would you write a song about a street with a name like that?

So, have you given any thought to the most common street name? Main? Wrong. Not even close. I'll give them to you in reverse order, like a Miss America contest. The fifth most common street name in America, according to postal service records, is . . . Lincoln!

The fourth most common name is . . . Oak. Third, Maple. The second most common is Washington. And the winner, the single most frequently used name for a street in all the U.S. is . . . Park! Park Street, Park Avenue, Park Terrace, Park Something, is the winner.

Of the twenty-five most common street names, seven are former Presidents. Nine are trees. Franklin is the only person's name in the first twenty-five who wasn't a President. And if you thought Broadway or Main were in there, you were really wrong. Main is thirty-second and Broadway isn't even in the first fifty.

Street names don't usually make much sense when you think about them. If a street is named Wolf Lane, it's usually been a hundred years since anyone saw a wolf around there. Very often there's no view of the bay from Bay View, no oak trees left on Oak Street and no hill anywhere around most of Hillside.

These days there's nothing interesting about the way a street gets its name. What happens most often is that a developer comes along and builds a bunch of houses all in a row (and they're all made of ticky-tack). At some point he realizes that if he's going to advertise them for sale they have to have an address. So he thinks up a cute name for the street and for the rest of its life that's what it's called.

Developers very often try to lend "class" to an area by calling it something other than a street. They call it a lane, a terrace or a circle. They'll call it Dogwood Lane hoping that they can ask more for a house on a lane than one on a street.

There is one mystery that remains unsolved in regard to street names in America. According to our count, Third Street was the seventeenth most popular street name. I accept that, but Second Street was nineteenth most common. And what about First Street? First Street was thirtieth!

Now what in the world ever happened to all the First Streets in cities that have Second and Third Streets? And how come there are more Thirds than Seconds? □

Adapted from "Street Names," *A Few Minutes with Andy Rooney,* by Andy Rooney. New York: Atheneum, 1981.

1. Which of the following would be the best title for the passage?

   (a) My Thoughts on American Street Names
   (b) How to Change Our Street Names
   (c) The Most Popular American Street Names
   (d) Great English Street Names

2. Which of the following is closest to the meaning of the word "originality," used in the second paragraph?

   (a) rich   (c) creativity
   (b) great   (d) foreign

3. Place a number from 1 to 5 next to each of the following United States street names to show how common it is according to the information in the passage.

   (a) _____ Lincoln   (d) _____ Maple
   (b) _____ Park   (e) _____ Washington
   (c) _____ Oak

4. The author got information about the most common street names in America from

   (a) a housing developer's office
   (b) traveling around the country
   (c) a national newspaper survey
   (d) postal service records

5. According to the passage, when a developer calls an area by a name other than "street," he hopes that

   (a) the buyers will be classy
   (b) the area will become a landmark
   (c) people will pay more for the houses
   (d) people won't notice the ticky-tack

6. Twelve street names mentioned in the passage are hidden in the puzzle. Circle each word you find, and then cross it off the list below. Street names can be read in any direction.

```
W  Y  M  A  P  L  E  N  T  S
O  A  K  L  P  A  R  K  E  B
E  W  S  E  C  O  N  D  S  K
D  D  E  H  E  R  K  D  N  L
I  A  M  A  I  N  J  R  U  I
S  O  R  L  C  N  I  I  S  N
L  R  N  O  T  E  G  H  E  C
L  B  L  D  F  A  U  T  X  O
I  Z  R  A  P  W  A  H  O  L
H  E  F  R  A  N  K  L  I  N
```

Broadway
Franklin
Hillside
Lincoln
Main
Maple
Oak
Park
Second
Sunset
Third
Washington

7. According to the author, calling a street Wolf Lane doesn't make much sense because

   (a) no family named Wolf lives there
   (b) there used to be wolves there
   (c) there are no wolves there now
   (d) there never were any wolves there

8. The author's attitude toward American street names in this passage could best be described as

   (a) nasty   **(c)** angry
   (b) joking   **(d)** patriotic

9. With which of the following statements about American street names would the author most likely agree?

    (a) Americans should be unhappy with most street names.
    (b) Americans should give more thought to naming their streets.
    (c) Americans should start renaming their streets right away.
    (d) Americans should use more English street names.

Check your answers on page 122.

10. **(For discussion)** Is there any street in your community that you would like to rename? Why do you think the present name is a bad one? What would you like the name to be? Why? Can you think of a really unusual street name in your area?

11. **(For discussion)** In the last two paragraphs, the author talks of a mystery he uncovered when he investigated street names. There are more Third Streets than Second Streets. Third Street is a slightly more popular name than Second Street. And First Street was all the way back at thirty in popularity. Can you think of any reason why? It <u>does</u> seem that if you have a Third Street, First and Second Streets should be there too. Can you think of any explanation for the "mystery"?

━━━━━━ *22* ━━━━━━━━━━━━━━━━━━━━━━━━━━━━

Here are some ways to protect yourself against frauds and swindles. In every community there are agencies that can help. Some of them are mentioned below. It's a good idea to look up the phone numbers of these helpers. Write the numbers down and keep them near your telephone. Then when you need help you'll know where to turn.

Buying by mail. You may find a lot of "junk mail" in your mailbox. Before you buy anything by mail, see if you can get a better deal at a local store. Beware of mail that offers an "easy" way to make money at home, or a "bargain" plot of land in some sunny place like Florida. You can check these offers with your local post office manager, the legal aid society, or a lawyer.

Buying at the door. Don't fall for gimmicks! Or for the "free" gift offers. When someone comes to your door and urges you to buy something right now, DON'T! Ask the salesperson to come back the next day. You can check on door-to-door sellers with your Better Business Bureau, the legal aid society, the local police station, or a community action center.

Signing your name. Before you sign your name on a contract or an agreement, be sure you can answer these two questions:

1. Do I understand everything it says?

2. Do I agree with everything it says?

If you answer "no" to either question, don't sign. If the contract is for something you really want, check it with a lawyer or the legal aid society.

Buying on credit. Don't be fooled by talk about "low" monthly payments. Find out the *total* amount you'll have to pay over the life of the loan. *Subtract* the actual price of the item you are buying. The *difference* is what you will be paying in interest. This is an extra charge to you. If it seems to be too much, check with a bank or a local community action center.

Health "cures" and health machines. Some are good and some are bad. Don't buy a health product or health machine just because someone says it's good. Check first with a doctor or at a local health clinic.

Eyeglasses and hearing aids. Do you think you need glasses or a hearing aid? Maybe you do. Or maybe someone in your family does. But you can't be sure until you are examined by your doctor or at your local health clinic. If you do need glasses or a hearing aid, don't buy them at a bargain price unless your doctor says it's all right. These aids need to be fitted properly. A bargain isn't a bargain if it won't help you the way it is supposed to.

Home repairs. If someone comes to your door and wants to fix up your home, be suspicious. Don't sign anything until you do these things:

1. Be sure the repairs are needed.

2. Get other estimates of the cost of doing the job.

3. Make sure the seller is legitimate.

4. Check with the Better Business Bureau.

If you do sign a contract, read it all! Make sure you are not mortgaging your home for a few dollars worth of repairs.

Some special tips:

- Don't be afraid to say "no." Don't let yourself be high-pressured into buying something you don't want or need.

- Get a receipt whenever you buy something. And be sure to read it all the way through.

- Don't be afraid to check on sellers. The only ones who will object to this are those who are trying to take advantage of you.

- Don't be afraid to call the mayor or the county commissioner. When you don't know who else to call, call the office of the mayor or the county commissioner. Someone there will be able to tell you where to get help.

- Talk with a bank officer. If you are going to use savings account money to make a purchase or close a business deal, talk first with an officer of your bank. He or she may have some pointers that will save you money, and maybe grief! □

Adapted from *Consumer Guide for Older People,* U.S. Department of Health, Education, and Welfare, March 1978.

1. The purpose of the passage is to alert people against

   (a) junk mail
   (b) door-to-door sellers
   (c) frauds and swindles
   (d) crooked contracts

2. The passage mentions all of the following as examples of possible fraud EXCEPT:

   (a) free gift offers at the door
   (b) easy ways to make money
   (c) low monthly payments
   (d) free legal aid

3. According to the passage, it is safe to sign a contract if you do any of the following things EXCEPT:

   (a) check with a lawyer
   (b) mortgage your home
   (c) call the Better Business Bureau
   (d) consult a bank officer

4. According to the passage, if you call the Better Business Bureau to check out a seller and the seller objects, the seller is probably

   (a) pressuring you to buy
   (b) selling you land
   (c) trying to cheat you
   (d) offering you free gifts

5. With which of the following statements about buying would the author probably agree?

   (a) Bargains can sometimes be expensive.
   (b) Most salespeople are dishonest.
   (c) Land in Florida is not a bargain.
   (d) Low monthly payments save you money.

6. From the passage you can conclude that when buying by mail, buyers CANNOT be

   (a) protected against fraud
   (b) sure about bargains
   (c) too suspicious
   (d) helped by the post office

7. Which of the following questions about fraud and swindles can you answer from the information in the passage?

   (a) How can I get my money back?
   (b) When will I receive my "free" gift?
   (c) Why didn't I get a receipt?
   (d) Where can I check on the seller?

8. Which of the following could best be used in place of the word "junk" in the second paragraph?

   (a) illegal   (c) trash
   (b) dishonest   (d) cheap

9. According to the passage, which of the following statements about interest payments is true?

   (a) They are the actual price of the item.
   (b) They are different from extra charges.
   (c) They may seem to be too much.
   (d) They may be subtracted from the price.

10. Find the HIDDEN MESSAGE:

   (a) Use the clues to list agencies that help buyers.
   (b) Circle the first letter of the first word. Then circle the second letter of the second word. Continue this pattern until you have circled the sixth letter of the sixth word.
   (c) The circled letters will reveal a HIDDEN MESSAGE.

   1. B _ _ _ _ _   B _ _ _ _ _ _ _
      B _ _ _ _ _ _   (agency to check on sellers)
   2. H _ _ _ _ _ _   C _ _ _ _ _ _   (place to check bargain eyeglasses)
   3. L _ _ _ _ _ _   (person to check contracts)
   4. L _ _ _ _ _   A _ _   (place for low-cost advice from a lawyer)
   5. M _ _ _ _ _   (elected head of the city)
   6. P _ _ _ _ _ _   (law enforcement officers)

Check your answers on page 124.

23

As one of the dumb, voiceless ones, I speak. One of the millions of immigrants beating, beating out their hearts at your gates for a breath of understanding.

America! From the other end of the earth from where I came, America was a land of living hope.

In this golden land of opportunity I would find my work that was denied me in the sterile village of my forefathers. Here I would be free from the dead drudgery for bread that held me down in Russia. For the first time in America, I'd cease to be a slave of the belly. My work would be the living joy of fullest self-expression.

I was in America, among the Americans, but not of them. No speech, no common language, no way to win a smile of understanding from them. Here I was with so much richness in me, but my mind was not wanted without the language.

My first job was as a servant in an Americanized family. Once, long ago, they came from the same village as I did. But they were so well-dressed, so well-fed, so successful in America, that they were ashamed to remember their mother tongue.

The best of me I gave them. Their house cares were my house cares. All that my soul hungered to give I put into the passion with which I scrubbed floors, scoured pots, and washed clothes. I was so grateful to mingle with the American people, to hear the music of the American language, that I never knew tiredness.

I could go on and on—not only with the work of the house, but work with my head—learning new words from the children, the grocer, the butcher, the iceman. I was not even afraid to ask for words from the policeman on the street. And every new word made me see new American things with American eyes. I felt like a Columbus, finding new worlds through every new word.

But words alone were only for the inside of me. On the outside I still looked like a steerage immigrant. I had to have clothes to forget myself that I'm a stranger yet. And so I had to have money to buy these clothes.

The month was up. I was so happy! Now I'd have money. *My own, earned* money. Money to buy a new shirt on my back—shoes on my feet. Maybe yet an American dress and hat!

In my imagination I already walked in my new American clothes. With money in my hands, I'd show them that I could look like an American in a day.

I trembled breathlessly for the minute I'd get the wages in my hand.

Before dawn I rose. I shined up the house like a jewel-box. I prepared breakfast and waited with my heart in my mouth.

The breakfast was over. And no word yet about my wages. I thought to myself, "Maybe they're so busy with their own things they forgot it's the day for my wages." Could they who have everything know what I was to do with my first American dollars? How could they, soaking in plenty, know the fierce hunger in me for the feel of my own, earned dollars? *My* dollars that would make me feel with everybody alike!

Lunch came. Lunch passed. It was dinner. And not a word yet about my wages.

I began to set the table. My head began to swim.

I couldn't stand it any longer. I dropped everything and rushed over to my American lady and gentleman.

"*Oi weh!* The money—my money—my wages!" I cried breathlessly.

Four cold eyes turned on me.

"Wages? Money?" The four eyes turned into hard stone as they looked me up and down. "Haven't you a comfortable bed to sleep, and three good meals a day? You're only a month here. Just came to America, and you already think about money. Wait 'til you're worth some money. What use are you without knowing English? You should be glad we even keep you here."

It went black for my eyes. I was so choked no words came to my lips. Even the tears went dry in my throat.

I left. Not a dollar for all my work. □

Condensed from "America and I," *Children of Loneliness,* by Anzia Yezierska. Originally published by Funk & Wagnalls, New York and London, 1923.

1. Which of the following best summarizes the author's main goal in America after her first job here?

    (a) learning to speak English
    (b) living independently
    (c) earning her own money
    (d) buying new clothes

2. Which of the following best describes the author's first employers?

    (a) They were born in America.
    (b) They often spoke in Russian.
    (c) They lived in a large house.
    (d) They were well-dressed.

3. All of the following describe the author's work EXCEPT:

    (a) ironing clothes   (c) scrubbing floors
    (b) preparing meals   (d) scouring pots

4. From the passage you can conclude that, in Russia, the author was

    (a) a slave   (c) a worker
    (b) hungry   (d) rich

5. According to the author, getting paid for her job in America depended on her

    (a) working harder   (c) dressing well
    (b) learning English   (d) staying longer

6. By the expression "mother tongue" in the fourth paragraph, the author means the language of her employers'

    (a) homeland   (c) new country
    (b) mother   (d) servants

7. According to the passage, the author wanted to buy new clothes in order to

   (a) forget who she was   (c) look like everyone else
   (b) appear to be rich   (d) keep her job

8. With which of the following statements about Americans would the author most likely agree?

   (a) They did not like her.
   (b) They would not hire her.
   (c) They did not want her here.
   (d) They did not understand her.

9. Which of the following phrases could best be substituted for "It went black for my eyes" in the last paragraph?

   (a) "I was very guilty."
   (b) "I was very upset."
   (c) "I was very embarrassed."
   (d) "I was very annoyed."

10. Which of the following words is closest in meaning to the word "sterile" in the second paragraph?

    (a) dead   (c) dirty
    (b) sad   (d) hungry

11. From the passage, you can infer that, for the author, learning English was like a

    (a) job   (c) pain
    (b) service   (d) discovery

12. The author's opinion of her employers in America is that they were

   (a) unfair   (c) forgetful
   (b) cheap   (d) dissatisfied

13. In this passage the word "dumb" in the first sentence most nearly means

   (a) ignorant   (c) hopeless
   (b) deaf   (d) silent

Check your answers on page 126.

24

The phone rang as I was saying good-bye to the children. It was my neighbor, Helen. Her voice was strained. "Have they gone yet?"

"Why? What's the matter?" I asked.

"It all happened so fast," she said. "Billy was almost out the door when I noticed he was only wearing his sneakers. Now he's been sick in bed all week, and there's still slush and snow on the ground. I could feel my anger rising, but I controlled myself. Very calmly I said, 'Billy, your boots.' He said, 'I don't need them; only babies wear boots.'

"Suddenly I found myself snarling at him. 'What is the matter with you? Are you stupid? Or are you deliberately trying to make yourself sick again? Just because some idiot fourth-grader decided that boots are out of style! Haven't you missed enough school this winter?'

"I threw the boots at his feet. He screamed, 'I hate you!' at the top of his lungs. I slapped him across the face! He shrieked, 'My ear! my ear!' And then I saw it—the imprint of my whole hand on his face and ear."

"Oh, no," I murmured. (My mind flashed back to that terrible incident last week between my son David and me. I had a strong urge to tell Helen about it, but something held me back.)

"Wait—there's more," she said. "Then he ran into the bathroom. He saw himself in the mirror and cried, 'Look what you did to me! I'm going to show everyone in school what you did to me!'"

That was too much for me. I gritted my teeth and decided to tell her. "I did something to David recently that I'm not exactly proud of either," I confessed.

"You hit him?" Helen asked hopefully.

"Worse," I said. "I called him 'the king of the rats.'"

"I feel better already," Helen sighed. "At least I'm not the only one who gets mad. What did David do to earn his title?"

"That's what's so strange. I don't even know what he did. It was what I *thought* he did. I heard Andy's voice from the bedroom pleading, 'David—STOP!' I started to dash in. Then I decided, no, I won't interfere, I'll let them work it out themselves. Then I heard Andy call out again. Only this time it sounded as if he were being strangled. And on top of it all, that big ox David was laughing gleefully. I went crazy. I charged into the room and grabbed him by the shirt collar. 'Do you know what you are?' I shouted. 'You're a rat. You're the king of the rats! And do you know what? You're no son of mine. Because you must have had a rat for a mother!' Then I pushed him away from me. He looked so little all of a sudden—so beaten. I've been sick about it ever since. I don't know why I said what I did. I only know that at the moment I couldn't stop myself. That was the most frightening part. It was as if there were two of me.

"I read about an experiment once. It was about rats and monkeys who had been angered. The scientists shocked them electrically, sometimes hit them on the head. They thought up all sorts of ways to frustrate them."

"What happened?" asked Helen.

"The poor creatures turned on each other—biting, tearing, clawing—sometimes to the death. It seemed that when the animals were angry enough—frustrated enough—certain bodily changes took place. These changes actually made it feel good for them to hurt or destroy each other."

"Are you suggesting," Helen said, "that when our children make us angry *we* behave like animals? That somehow we've got to attack them because it feels good? In that case, there's no hope for us!" □

Adapted from *Liberated Parents, Liberated Children* by Adele Faber and Elaine Mazlish. New York: Grosset & Dunlap, 1974. Pp. 173–176.

1. The author called her son "the king of the rats" because he

   (a) wouldn't wear his boots
   (b) screamed "I hate you!" at her
   (c) hit Billy on the ear
   (d) seemed to be hurting Andy

2. The women are talking about what happens when they get

   (a) angry with their children
   (b) tired of their children
   (c) unhappy with their children's school work
   (d) careless about being parents

3. Helen got angry at her son because he

   (a) had been sick all week
   (b) was wearing his sneakers
   (c) refused to wear his boots
   (d) screamed at her first

4. What can you conclude were the author's reasons for not telling Helen her own story right away?

   (a) She was afraid of Helen's reaction.
   (b) She was trying to forget the fight.
   (c) She was too ashamed to tell her.
   (d) She was still too angry to talk about it.

5. When the author got angry she didn't ask her sons what they were doing because she

   (a) wanted to let them work it out by themselves
   (b) didn't want to get angry
   (c) wanted to talk to Helen first
   (d) was trying an experiment

6. Which of the following best expresses the meaning of the word "gleefully" in the twelfth paragraph?

(a) childishly   (c) violently
(b) happily   (d) hopefully

7 Which of the following best describes how Helen probably felt after hearing the author's story?

(a) angry   (c) jealous
(b) hopeful   (d) relieved

8. In the fourth paragraph from the end of the passage, the author starts to tell Helen of an experiment she had read about. The purpose of that experiment was to find out what happened when rats and monkeys

(a) scratched and bit
(b) got angry
(c) attacked their babies
(d) felt good

9. What were the results of the experiment on anger described by the author?

(a) Mothers stopped hitting their children.
(b) Mothers felt good when they hit their children.
(c) Animals stopped biting and clawing each other.
(d) Animals felt good when they hurt each other.

10. The author would probably describe anger as something

(a) to learn how to handle
(b) to be ashamed of
(c) that should always be controlled
(d) that can never be controlled

Check your answers on page 129.

11. **(For discussion)** Think about Helen's fight with her son Billy. What should she do if the same problem happens again?

12. **(For discussion)** Think of a time when you got very angry with someone. Did you have a good reason to be angry? What did you do first? Then what happened? Were you happy with the way things came out? If not, can you think of something you could have done differently to bring about a better result?

13. **(For discussion)** In the last paragraph, Helen wonders if people behave like animals when they get angry because it "feels good." Do you think people feel good when they hurt their children in anger? Why or why not? Do you agree with Helen that "in that case, there's no hope for us"? Explain your answer.

25

As a licensed driver, you must know and obey the rules of the road. While every state has different rules for safe driving, there are many that are the same everywhere. Let's take a quick review of them by taking an imaginary journey. We'll start in a home driveway in a village and go to a nearby city. Of course, we cannot cover all of the rules, or all of the exceptions to them. For further information consult your Driver's Manual or your state's motor vehicle and traffic laws.

All set? Let's go!

As you start the car out of the driveway, you must stop and yield the right-of-way to pedestrians on the sidewalk. Then you must yield the right-of-way to cars on the street before you can enter the street.

You signal that you are turning onto the street. Then make a right turn and proceed down the street. As you go, keep to the right. Operate your vehicle at a speed which is reasonable and within the speed limit as posted.

The first intersection you reach has no traffic lights or signs. As you reach this intersection, another car approaches down a street to your left. If you both reach the intersection at the same time, and there is no immediate danger, your car has the right-of-way because it is on the right.

The next intersection is controlled by a flashing red light. This means come to a full stop, in the same way that you would for a STOP sign. Stop your car at the stop line or crosswalk. When the way is clear, proceed with caution through the intersection.

As you reach the outskirts of the village, you come to a rotary traffic circle that leads to the main highway to the city. Before you enter the traffic circle, yield the right of way to cars already moving in the circle. When the way is clear, you can enter the circle. Continue around it to your exit, signal your turn, and leave.

Now you are on the main highway to the city. It is a four-lane, divided highway. Here you can increase your speed to 55 miles per hour. This is the legal maximum speed in most states, unless another speed limit is posted. Keep a reasonable distance between your car and the vehicle ahead of you. This will help you avoid hitting the car ahead if it slows or stops. Keep in the right-hand lane except in the following cases:

1. when overtaking and passing a vehicle, pedestrian, animal, or anything else that is blocking the right-hand lane

2. when preparing to make a left turn

After a short distance on this highway, you signal your turn and exit onto a two-lane road that leads to the city. On this road, the opposing lines of traffic are divided by pavement markings. A double, solid line prohibits passing. A solid line with a broken line on one side means that cars on the broken line side may pass. A single broken line indicates that cars going in either direction may pass.

When you pass another car, you must return to the correct lane after you are safely clear of the vehicle you have overtaken. You may never pass—from either direction—a school bus which is stopped to load or unload passengers.

As you reach the city, reduce your speed to the posted speed limit. At the first intersection, you want to make a left turn. Signal your turn. When the light turns green, proceed into the intersection. Wait for oncoming traffic to clear before making your turn.

At the next intersection, a police officer is directing traffic. She signals you through even though the light is red, and you must obey her instructions. As you pass through the intersection you hear the siren of an emergency vehicle. You must immediately pull out of the intersection and pull as close to the side of the road as possible until the emergency vehicle has passed.

You find a parking space near your destination and pull into it. Your trip, and this review of the rules of the road, are both over. □

Adapted from *How Well do you Know the Rules of the Road?*, New York State Department of Motor Vehicles, 1981.

1. The purpose of the passage is to give drivers the

   (a) rules for driving in every state
   (b) road map for an imaginary trip
   (c) basic rules for safe driving
   (d) traffic laws in their own state

2. Which of the following words could best be used instead of "yield" in the third paragraph?

   (a) drive   (c) direct
   (b) give   (d) run

3. According to the passage, your car has the right of way at an intersection without traffic lights or signs if

   (a) it is to the right of another car
   (b) if it is to the left of another car
   (c) the car on the left has already crossed
   (d) a car is coming in the opposite direction

4. The author says that when a car comes to an intersection controlled by a flashing red light, it must

    (a) slow down and wait for a flashing yellow light
    (b) slow down and then cross when the way is clear
    (c) come to a full stop and then cross when the way is clear
    (d) come to a full stop and wait for a flashing yellow light

5. Below are some markings you are likely to find on a road. You are driving a car in the direction indicated by the arrow. You would like to pass the slow-moving car in front of you. On the line next to each letter, write YES if you <u>may</u> pass the car in front of you. Write NO if you <u>may not</u> pass.

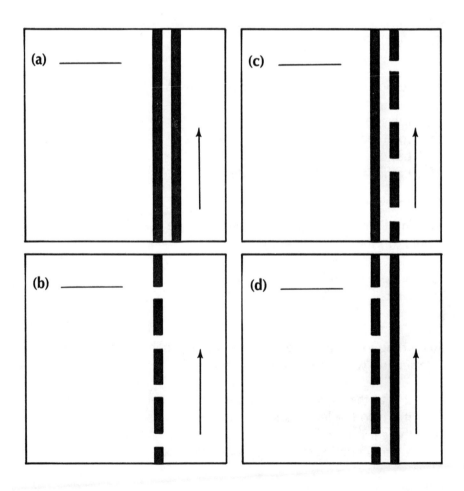

6. The word "destination" in the last paragraph means your

   (a) home   (c) first stop
   (b) job   (d) last stop

7. According to the passage you can infer that a man driving at a speed of 25 m.p.h. on a country road where the speed limit is 45 m.p.h. is probably

   (a) driving carefully   (c) driving unsafely
   (b) an elderly driver   (d) a student driver

8. According to the passage, when a traffic officer gives instructions, a driver must immediately

   (a) obey even if it means going through a red light
   (b) not obey if it means going through a red light
   (c) look to see what the other drivers are doing
   (d) look to see if an emergency vehicle is coming

9. According to the passage, the legal maximum speed limit in most states is _____ miles per hour.

   (a) 60   (c) 35
   (b) 55   (d) 65

10. According to the passage, you may not pass

    (a) a car that is blocking the right-hand lane
    (b) a car on a city street
    (c) another vehicle that is going in the same direction
    (d) a school bus that has stopped for passengers

11. Unscramble the letters below to find the names of the different kinds of roadways mentioned in this passage.

ETRETS   _ _ _ _ _ _

AYHGIHW   _ _ _ _ _ _ _ _

AIVDWREY   _ _ _ _ _ _ _ _ _

ICFRAFT ELCICR   _ _ _ _ _ _ _   _ _ _ _ _ _ _

Check your answers on page 131.

12. **(For discussion)**   You are riding home with a friend from a party. He's driving and had a few drinks. He's not really drunk, but he's not paying attention to the rules of the road. How would you handle this situation?

Answers and Explanations

1. **(b-main idea)** The main point the author is trying to make is that the risk of premature death is greater for smokers than for non-smokers. The passage gives many reasons why this is true. Two of these reasons are that smokers are in greater danger of cancer and lung disease, but these are just two of the diseases mentioned. The statistics on men aged 40–69 show one example of the greater risk of premature death to people who smoke.

2. **(c-main idea)** The author would agree with research that says that smoking is a life-and-death issue. The passage sets out the dangers of smoking, and the research that supports the conclusion that smoking is dangerous. It tells you about the advantages of quitting. The graph does show that the number of deaths from lung cancer in women has risen. But it does not say that smoking is more dangerous for women than men (b), or that smoking causes all of this cancer (d). The first paragraph says that the days when people thought smoking was good for your nerves (a) are gone.

3. **(b-vocabulary)** The word "early" could be used in place of "premature." Look at the paragraph. It talks about people dying from diseases caused by smoking. They might have lived longer if they hadn't smoked. Because they did smoke, they died early. "Expected" is the opposite of early, and nothing is said about their deaths being painful or happening suddenly.

4. **(c-supporting detail)** According to the passage, just one cigarette will speed up your heartbeat. This information is found in the third paragraph. Smoking also affects the cilia, the skin, and the blood, but not in the ways listed in the other answer choices.

5. **(a-conclusion)** From the information in the graph, you can conclude that more women smoked cigarettes. The graph tells you that while fewer adults as a whole were smoking in 1980, more cigarettes were sold. The graph also tells you that the number of women with lung cancer rose dramatically in the same period of time. The passage clearly states that smokers have a greatly increased chance of getting lung cancer. Since the number of women with lung cancer increased

at the same time the number of cigarettes smoked did, you can conclude that more women were smoking. There is no information in the graph about doctors *(d)*, the number of low-tar cigarettes made *(c)*, or the number of adults with lung cancer *(b)*.

6. **(d-vocabulary)** The word "paralyzes" most nearly means "stops." The next sentence says that cilia are "hairlike." The paragraph also says that they move about to keep your lungs clean. If smoking stops the cilia from doing their job, it must stop them from moving. Speeding the cilia up or moving them wouldn't stop them from cleaning the lungs. There is nothing in the passage about their height.

7. **(b-supporting detail)** According to the graph, the percent of adults who smoke has not increased. In 1964, 53 percent of adults smoked. In 1980, only 38 percent smoked. This is a decrease of 15 percent. The graph does show that more women died of lung cancer, the cigarette industry spent more money, and more cigarettes were smoked per year. "More" of anything is an increase.

8. **(d-inference)** You can infer that once you stop smoking, your lungs will begin to clean themselves. The third paragraph says that smoking paralyzes the cilia. The cilia clean the lungs. The sixth paragraph says that the minute you stop smoking, your body will go to work to repair the damage caused by smoking. From this you can figure out that when you stop smoking, the cilia will start to repair themselves. Then the cilia can do their job. This does not mean that you will automatically live 20 years longer, or never go to the hospital. The third paragraph says that smoking lowers your skin temperature. If you quit, it will go up.

2

1. **(c-main idea)** The best title for the passage would be "An Easy Energy Saver." The first paragraph says that you can lose energy through the spaces under doors. It also tells you that making something to block this space and save energy is easy. The rest of the passage tells you how to make this energy saver. You have to do some sewing and you do use old rags, but those things are just part of making the draft guard. The passage tells you one way to <u>keep</u> your home warm. It does not tell you how to <u>make</u> it warm in the first place.

2. **(d-supporting detail)** According to the diagrams, the material should be cut so it is slightly longer than the width of the door. The first instruction in figure A tells you it should be the width of the door "plus several inches." There is no information in the drawings to support the other options.

3. **(d-inference)** The author would probably agree that you can spend less money on heating bills and still stay warm. The passage tells you one thing you can make to help you save energy. If you save energy, your heating bills will be smaller. The author would not agree with the other options. Using this draft guard is just one thing you can do to save money on heat. Nothing is said about buying a new house. And if you're losing energy because of lots of drafts, it may not matter how much you spend on heat.

4. **(b-conclusion)** Gravel can be used instead of sand. Gravel is about as dense and heavy as sand, and can take any shape. The other substances can also be shaped, but they aren't dense or heavy enough. The draft guard must be dense and heavy so it won't be moved by air and air can't pass through it.

5. **(a-inference)** You should not sew all sides of the tube before it's turned inside-out because the tube must be filled before it is closed. The last paragraph tells you that the tube should not be closed completely until it's filled. Nothing is said about the fabric tearing *(b)*. The last thing you do is place the tube by the door *(c)*, and the length and width of the fabric have nothing to do with how it's sewn.

6. **(c-conclusion)** The draft guard saves energy because it fills up an opening. The first paragraph explains how energy is lost through the spaces under doors. The draft guard blocks these openings because it's filled with dense material. Nothing in the passage suggests that the width of the fabric has anything to do with whether the draft guard works or not. It could be 6" or 7" wide. The passage does not say that sand reflects cold air or stores hot air.

7. **(b-vocabulary)** The word "effective" most nearly means "good" in this passage. Look at the way the word is used. The passage says that drafts are a problem, and shows you how to make something to stop them. The author would not bother telling you about it if it didn't work. There is nothing strange about a draft guard. While the guard may be strong and quick to make, these are just two reasons why it's good.

8. **(b-style/tone)** The tone of the passage sounds most like a textbook. The passage and the diagrams explain how to do something. The passage has no people speaking, and does not tell a story. Plays and

novels usually contain both these things. A speech usually tries to convince you of the speaker's opinion. The passage doesn't try to do this.

<h1 align="center">3</h1>

1. **(c-inference)** Lorena would probably say that for a marriage to work out, the most important thing is that the man must be strong and take charge. The first sentence says that she tried all kinds of ways to make John a "man." The third paragraph tells you that John was a "boy," but that Lorena wanted him to be the "master." It also says their marriage failed. From this, you can infer that if John had taken charge as the "master," Lorena thinks their marriage would have worked. The third paragraph also says that Lorena blamed John as well as herself for their problems. So she wouldn't agree with answer choice d. There is nothing in the passage about John's job (a), and although Lorena prays (b), she does not say that it helped her marriage.

2. **(b-vocabulary)** The word "coax" could be used in place of the word "cajole." You can see this from the way the word "cajole" is used. The other things the sentence says that Lorena was doing are all different ways of trying to get someone to do what you want. This is also the meaning of the word "coax." If you cheat or ignore someone, that person will not do what you want. In Lorena's situation, making jokes would not have gotten her what she wanted.

3. **(d-inference)** You can infer that Lorena's new prayers asked God to help her make John stronger. In her prayers she tells God, "You know what I need." In the next paragraph, Lorena says that it was her job to change her husband. From this you can figure out that Lorena was asking God to help her do what she thought was her job. She had already realized that making John a good husband and father (a) was not God's job, so she wasn't asking Him to do this. She says later that both she and John were at fault, and she was still married when all these things were happening.

4. **(c-conclusion)** When Lorena uses the words, "His pants had a crease, mine had a ruffle," she means that she had to run the family. "Wearing the pants" in a family is an expression that means "being in control." Years ago, it was only men that wore pants. Lorena is

unhappy with John because he won't act the way she thinks a man should act. He won't become the master of the house. Lorena is saying that <u>she</u> was the one that acted like a man and took control. She "wore the pants." But this is only an expression. All the other answer choices are talking about real clothes, and the passage doesn't say anything about real clothes.

5. **(Word problem)** Some of the words hidden in "otherwise" are:

other	the	her	ere	rise	wise	ire	see
owe	three	here	ewe	row	wit	it	set
ore	there	hoe	ewer	rot	woe	its	sew
	their	his		rose	whet		sir
	tow	hot			wet		sere
	tower	how			wish		sit
	tree	hit			wire		stir
	tire	hose					stow
	two	hew					show
		hire					shower
		hoist					shot
							stew
							shoe
							sire

━━━━━━━ **4** ━━━━━━━━━━━━━━━━━━━━━━━━━━━━

1. **(c-main idea)** The author is most concerned with explaining why women stay with men who beat them. The passage presents a list of reasons why the author thinks this sometimes happens. She is trying to correct a mistake she thinks the newspaper has made. She does not say why women marry men who beat them *(b)*. We are not told why men beat women *(a)*. The author doesn't believe beaten women have a bad opinion of themselves *(d)*. In the last sentence of the first paragraph, she calls this idea "hogwash."

2. **(d-supporting detail)** The author does not say that doctors helped her husband to stop beating her. In the seventh paragraph, in fact, she says that doctors did not believe her husband beat her. In the last paragraph she says she has bitter memories of doctors who told her that she must enjoy being hit. All of the other answer choices *(a)*, *(b)*, and *(c)* are all reasons why women stay with men who abuse them.

3. **(c-inference)** The author wrote her letter to the editor because she disagreed with what the newspaper said. You can find this in the first paragraph. She doesn't say anything about men in general. Since she didn't sign her name, she couldn't want to embarrass her husband. To be embarrassed, he would have to know that his wife wrote the letter. The letter is filled with unpleasant things. There is not much chance she enjoyed writing it.

4. **(b-conclusion)** The author would probably agree with the statement that beaten women need someplace to go. One reason the author stayed with her husband is that she had nowhere to go. She says this in the fifth paragraph. She also says here that she <u>lost</u> her friends *(c)*, and that the police told her that her violent husband was <u>her</u> problem *(a)*. She says in the seventh paragraph that doctors didn't believe her, so they were no help at all *(d)*.

5. **(a-vocabulary)** The word "pestering" most nearly means "bothering." Look at the fifth paragraph. The author says that her friends could not "put up" with her husband for long. This means he was bothering them. Later on, she says she was told that she had no right to bother the police with her husband. Yelling, lying, and beating her up are all things her husband did, but she isn't talking about these things in the fifth paragraph.

6. **(b-inference)** You can infer that the author's name wasn't printed because she was afraid of her husband. The whole letter is about how her husband hurt her. At the end, she says that she was lucky to get away. From these facts, you can conclude that she is still afraid and that she doesn't want him to know where she lives. Although some people who don't sign letters are lying, it is plain the author has a good reason for keeping her name secret. There is no way to know if she is still married. She is not playing a joke.

5

1. **(d-supporting detail)** The F.B.I. accused some of the judges after investigating them for four years. Three judges were accused. You can find this information in the fourth paragraph.

2. **(c-supporting detail)** According to the passage, before the police can use bugs and wiretaps, they must have a good reason. You can find this in the fourth paragraph. The other options are wrong. If

there is a good reason the Supreme Court and the Constitution support the use of wiretaps, so the Constitution wouldn't have to be changed. They would not have to ask the Supreme Court. There is nothing in the passage that says the F.B.I. would have to ask a judge.

3. **(b-inference)** You can conclude that the F.B.I. agents were most concerned with making arrests. Most of the judges were honest. But the agents weren't interested in honest judges. The agents did not take the time to pick out judges they had a reason to think were dishonest. They bugged and tried to bribe them all. The fourth paragraph says that police must have a reason to think a person is breaking the law. Only then can they plant a bug. That is the law. Since they went ahead without a reason, they were clearly not supporting the law. They thought that if they listened in, and got some judges to take bribes, they could make lots of arrests.

4 **(b-conclusion)** According to the passage, when the F.B.I. agents tried to bribe the judges, the agents were acting illegally. Trying to bribe the judges was probably entrapment, because the judges never asked for money. It was the agents who tried again and again to give it to the judges. Most of the judges were honest, and the F.B.I. was breaking the law, not enforcing it *(a)*. There is nothing in the passage about the agents' orders *(c)*. Since only three of the judges took the bribes, the agents had no evidence *(d)*. And since entrapment is not legal, the agents cannot use facts gathered in that way in a trial.

5 **(c-vocabulary)** The word "sham" means "fake." Look at the fifth paragraph. Right before the author calls the cases "sham," he calls them phony. Later he says that the courts were overcrowded with real cases. From this, you can figure out that the F.B.I.'s cases were fakes. The F.B.I. did keep them secret, and many people do think they were unfair, but these words don't fit the context. The cases were not about real criminals.

6. **(a-conclusion)** You can conclude that if more judges had taken bribes, people wouldn't have been as critical. The last paragraph says that when real criminals, like drug smugglers or killers are caught, the F.B.I.'s methods are not often questioned. You can conclude that if more of the judges had been really dishonest, too, people would feel the same way. But people saw good judges being treated like criminals. This is what made them critical. The passage says more undercover operations are planned. There is nothing in the passage about judges in other cities or people wanting more proof about the three judges the F.B.I. did accuse.

7. **(d-vocabulary)** You can conclude that the word "persistent" means "stubborn." Look at the fifth paragraph. It says that when a judge

refused a bribe, the agents kept trying. Sometimes they would try many times. The agents just would not believe the judges were honest. This is stubborn thinking. "Dishonest" and "sneaky" may fit some of the other things the F.B.I. did, but they don't fit the actions called "persistent." There is nothing to suggest that the F.B.I. agents were "confused."

8. **(c-main idea)** The author would probably agree that the best way for the F.B.I. to support the law would be to always obey it themselves. The author talks about the F.B.I.'s methods. He asks, "Did they go too far?" He wonders whether these methods were legal or not. If the F.B.I. went too far and broke the law, they could not be supporting it, too. It's hard to think of people honestly supporting the law if they are also breaking it. The author would probably think that watching people (d), and acting like crooks (b), would be going too far. He says that bugs and wiretaps are legal if there is a good reason to use them (a).

6

1. **(c-main idea)** The best title for the passage would be "Where Are They When You Need Them?" In the first paragraph the author says she worked all her life and paid her taxes. She has never asked for help. When she finally needs help, she can't get it. This is the main point of the passage. You are not really told <u>how</u> to apply for welfare (b). Taxes are mentioned only in the first paragraph (d). The author <u>has</u> done men's jobs (a), but that is not the main point of the passage.

2. **(b-inference)** You can infer that the author believes the person at the Hub Center was not really interested in her. She told him that she and her husband George were starving and had no money for rent or medicine. All he gave her was a note to get a sandwich. He didn't say much, so he wasn't making fun of her. She may have felt cheated and lied to, but nothing in the passage says that the young man really did either of these things.

3. **(c-conclusion)** When the author goes to the welfare office, she needs help because she has to take care of George. The second paragraph tells you this. George had a stroke. The author had to quit her job to take care of him. Stroke victims need a lot of care. The author knew she would need help so that she and George could get

by. Several times she says she has worked all her life. She says that she was forced to stop working; she never says she wants to quit. She and George had no money, so they couldn't move out of her son's house. She went to the welfare office before she went to Hub Center.

4. **(c-vocabulary)** A punch press is most likely a factory machine. You can figure this out by looking at the context. In the first sentence, the author says that she worked in factories. From this you can guess that the machines the author used are used in factories. She never mentions farms, or working on a farm. Screwdrivers and electric drills are two other tools she has used.

5. **(d-conclusion)** You can conclude that the author couldn't get help from welfare because she and her husband lived with her son. In the third paragraph, the author says that the welfare office told her that her son would have to take care of them. She and George would have to move out of their son's house before the welfare agency would help. The other answer choices aren't supported by the passage. She couldn't work because she had to take care of George. He was very ill and had just come out of the hospital, and could not work.

6. **(b-inference)** The author thought she should get government benefits because she had paid her taxes. Look at the first paragraph. She says there that she has paid her taxes into government programs and she now needs help. The author felt she should get government benefits because she worked and paid her share. She isn't too old to work, and is not complaining about her job. She feels she should get help because she needs it and earned it, not just because she asked.

7. **(d-supporting detail)** The person at Hub Center filled out a form so that the author could get a sandwich. You can find this information in the fourth paragraph. The other answer choices are all things that the author needed but did _not_ get.

8. **(b-style/tone)** When the author talks about asking for help from the government, her tone is desperate. In the second paragraph, the author tells you about her problems. She tells you that she finally realized she needed help in solving them. As big as her problems were, she says she had never asked for help before. She waited until she was desperate and had nowhere else to turn. She does not sound frightened (a). She sounds angry and helpless. In the first paragraph, she says that she worked all her life and got no help when she needed it, so she is not lazy (c). Since she got no help, she would not be relieved (d).

7

1. **(d-main idea)** The main idea of the passage is that people who make the American Dream come true are hard workers who know what they want. Look at the last two paragraphs. The young woman, Laura Fan, knows what she wants to be. She says she'll give it her "best shot." This could go for any of the people mentioned in the passage. When they talk about their lives and their work, they all use words like "explore," "challenges," and "dedication." These words are all clues to how these people became successful. They all knew what they wanted and worked hard to get it. The passage doesn't say that Alger was poor (a). Some people in the passage were born in other countries (b), but others were not. Most people would call earning $50,000 a year a success (c), but the people in the passage measure success by other things besides money, too.

2. **(b-supporting detail)** The American Dream may best be described as going from rags to riches. Look at the third paragraph. It says that most Americans still believe in the American Dream. The last sentence says the same people thought the poorest child could rise to riches. From these statements, you can figure out what the author means by the American Dream. Many people want to become American citizens (d). Some want to work for big companies (c). Some people also dream about money (a). But these things are just some parts of the whole American Dream.

3. **(d-supporting detail)** All of the following names belong on the list EXCEPT Horatio Alger. The fourth paragraph tells you that Alger was a writer. The other people are successful people who have led lives like some of the people in Alger's books.

4. **(c-inference)** The author most likely would agree with the statement that you can take charge of your life. The author believes that people can get what they want if they work hard. That means people must take charge of their lives. The passage does not mention luck (a) or college (b). Carlos Arboleya was not born in America (d), and he is very successful.

5. **(b-vocabulary)** You can conclude that "I'll give it my best shot" means, "I'll try as hard as I can." When Laura Fan says this, she is talking about her goals in life, and how hard they will be to reach. But she is going to try. She says if you "put your mind" to getting something done, you can do it. From this, you can tell that she will try very hard to get what she wants. Answer choices (a) and (c) are

not things Fan would say. These statements are the words of a person who has given up. To be a lawyer, Fan will have to finish college *(d)*, but she isn't talking about college here.

6. **(b-tone/style)** The style of the passage is most like a newspaper. Newspapers are mostly concerned with facts. The passage is a collection of facts. In the second paragraph, the author talks about a poll that says that 81 percent of the people asked still believed in the American Dream. The passage goes on to tell you some facts about people who have made the American Dream come true. A speech tries to convince you of something, and doesn't have to be made up of facts. Plays and novels aren't usually about real people.

7. **(c-conclusion)** You can conclude that Horatio Alger's novels are about poor people getting rich. Read the second and third paragraphs. The second paragraph says that people still believe in success stories of the kind Alger wrote. It says they still believe the poorest child can rise to riches. From this, you can conclude Alger wrote about poor people becoming successful. The novels are not <u>only</u> about poor people *(a)*, or <u>only</u> about rich people *(d)*, or about rich people getting richer *(b)*.

8. **(Word jumble)**

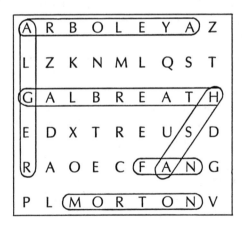

1. **(d-main idea)** The author is trying to convince readers that by studying computers at home they can become skilled amateurs. She says that you can learn to understand, or become familiar with, computers

at home. She tells you that she is not a computer expert *(a)*. The passage does not imply that you will become a computer programmer *(c)*, or that you will be able to write about computers *(b)*.

2. **(a-supporting detail)** The author does not know more than her co-workers. She tells you that she works with people who know a great deal <u>more</u> than she does. In the first paragraph she also states that she never learned much about science or math *(b)*. She does know enough to share her knowledge with others *(d)*. In fact, she has been studying at home for three years, so she must know many things *(c)*.

3. **(c-supporting detail)** The fifth paragraph states that a computer is all logical. The author says that learning it is easier than you fear, so it is not difficult *(d)* or a secret *(b)*. She found that engineering and electronics were puzzling *(a)*, but not computers.

4. **(a-inference)** You can conclude that in order to write about computers, the author studied very hard. In the second paragraph, she writes about her two years of hard work. She tells you how she sat down with the computer day after day, and night after night. The author did not understand electronics *(c)*. There is nothing in the passage that says she really took a course *(b)* or that she learned from other people *(d)*.

5. **(b-conclusion)** The author believes that one of the most useful things about many people who understand computers is that they are eager to help. The fifth paragraph states that many people will always be happy to help you. This means that they are eager to do so. The author states that computers are logical, not the people who use them *(a)*. The author doesn't say what these people do for a living *(d)*, or that they are teaching computer courses *(c)*.

6. **(d-conclusion)** You can conclude that the author thinks that a person who took a computer course would learn about computers the easy way. In the third paragraph, the author says that taking a course is the best way to learn about computers. In the second paragraph, she says that learning her way was costly in personal terms. You can conlude from this that if she had taken a course, things would have been easier. Although she says that a course is the <u>best</u> way to learn, she doesn't say it's any faster *(a)*. People have different speeds of learning. The author does not say anythng about thinking like a computer *(c)*. She just says that you should learn the rules. She says that her co-workers know more than she does, but she doesn't say a course will teach you as much as they know *(b)*.

7. **(d-conclusion)** The author tells you that she can use a computer to do work that she gets paid for. This shows you that she can earn money at home with a computer. She says that working with a

computer is <u>like</u> taking in typing *(b)*. This doesn't mean it's the same thing. Making your home into an office *(c)* and doing schoolwork *(a)* are not mentioned in the passage.

8. **(a-vocabulary)** The word "ordeal" means something that is difficult. The author tells how hard she worked over a two-year period. The phrase "at such personal cost" tells you she went through personal hardships to learn about computers. This period of time was not boring for the author *(b)*, because she was learning. Nothing in the passage tells you she was frightened *(c)* of learning about computers.

9. **(Word problem)** HOME COMPUTER:
   (a) CHUM   **(b)** POEM   **(c)** TORE

9

1. **(c-main idea)** The main idea of the passage is that people who join groups should be active and responsible. The passage gives you some ideas on how to make a group successful. All these ideas need active people who are willing to do their share to make them work. The passage ends by telling you that everyone benefits if all the members do their jobs, so answer choice *d* is not true. The second paragraph says that people join groups to help themselves. This doesn't mean they are only thinking about themselves *(a)*. It means they understand that the best way for people to help themselves is to help each other. Nothing in the passage suggests that people join groups just to have someplace to go *(b)*.

2. **(a-supporting detail)** According to the author, a person joins any group because he or she has found the answer to the question, "What's in it for me?" You can find this information in the second paragraph. It says people join groups because of the things they will gain. The questions listed in answer choices *(b)*, *(c)*, and *(d)* are all things people would ask themselves before joining <u>certain</u> kinds of groups. But only answer choice *(a)* gives a question someone would ask before joining <u>any</u> group at all.

3. **(d-supporting detail)** According to the passage, being a responsible group member does <u>not</u> include talking and always being quiet at meetings. The fourth piece of advice listed is to speak up. The author says that if you don't, a few people who like to talk will run the

group. Answer choices *(a)*, *(b)*, and *(c)* are all things the author says you should do.

4. **(d-conclusion)** You can conclude that because people act together in a group all might want to help the community. The first paragraph lists some things that groups can do. These are some reasons people join groups. Many of these things would help a community. In the last paragraph, the author says that groups can help people and improve neighborhoods. The other answer choices are things that can happen in a group. But it's not very likely that the group members want these things to happen, or that these are reasons people would join. The passage gives some ideas for preventing these things.

5. **(c-conclusion)** The sentence that could best be used in place of "There is strength in numbers" is "A group can do more than one person alone." You can figure this out from the context. Look at the last paragraph. The sentence just before says that people working as a group can do things they couldn't do alone. This means that a group is stronger than one person. The paragraph isn't talking about strong people—answer choices *(a)* and *(d)*—or money *(b)*.

6. **(b-vocabulary)** The word "gripe" most nearly means "complaint." Look at the way the word is used. The speaker doesn't know what's happening at the meeting and wants someone to tell him. He is unhappy, and is complaining about it to the group. The speaker is not making a speech *(d)* or quoting a saying *(c)*. A dialogue *(a)* is a conversation between two people.

⟨⟨⟨⟨⟨⟨ *10* ⟩⟩⟩⟩⟩⟩⟩⟩⟩⟩⟩⟩⟩⟩⟩⟩⟩⟩⟩⟩⟩⟩⟩⟩⟩⟩⟩⟩⟩⟩⟩

1. **(c-main idea)** The main purpose of the passage is to show that people have the power inside themselves to change things. The author says in the seventh paragraph, "If I could get the park for them, they would believe it's possible to do other things." The passage does not say people should only fight Bethlehem Steel *(a)* or always fight big companies *(b)*. The author does not say people have the power to take over steel companies. His point is that people have the power to change some of the things a big company does.

2. **(a-detail)** The author thinks the country is "sick." He says this in the first paragraph. He sees this sickness when he looks at the "daily injustices" of life here, and at poor people who have been "left out" of the system. An "injustice" is the opposite of something "fair" *(b)*.

A "loving" country *(d)* would not leave poor people out of its society. The author doesn't say he thinks the country is dangerous *(c)*. If he did think this, he would probably be working to help people protect themselves from danger.

3. **(c-supporting detail)** In the fifth paragraph, the author says that most people don't fight back against big companies because they think the companies will win. The people in the passage showed you that people <u>do</u> have the time *(a)* and energy *(c)* to fight. But people must believe that they have a chance of winning. The people in the passage did not think Bethlehem Steel was right. There is no reason to believe they think any differently from other people.

4. **(b-conclusion)** The author suggests that after the people of Pike County forced Bethlehem Steel to build a park, they would believe it's possible to do other things. The sixth paragraph makes the point that once people succeed, their confidence increases. The author does not suggest that the people will think of Bethlehem Steel as their friend. In fact, he believes Bethlehem Steel will show it is not their friend if they make other demands *(a)*. He does not expect the people to thank the steel company for building a park *(c)*. The company only built the park because the people forced them to. He hopes the people will go on and force Bethlehem Steel to stop strip mining *(d)*.

5. **(b-inference)** You can conclude that the people of Pike County can fight for their rights if they are organized. That is what the author taught them to do. Once they are organized, they might be able to fight any big company, but winning is never a sure thing *(a)*. And they would have to be organized <u>first</u>. Given confidence and organization, they could fight Bethlehem Steel again, but once more, it's still possible they might lose *(c)*. Now that they've organized, they might choose a leader other than the author *(d)*.

6. **(c-inference)** The National Council of Churches probably put pressure on Bethlehem Steel. In the seventh paragraph, the author says he wanted the National Council of Churches to start "calling up, writing, and hounding Bethlehem." These are all ways of putting on pressure. In the next paragraph, he says that this is exactly what happened. Bethlehem started thinking the pressure was a "pain." It was the author and the people of Pike County who called up the "big wheels," not the Council *(a)*. The Council did not collect money for the park *(b)*. Bethlehem Steel paid for it all. The author does not say who paid his salary *(d)*.

7. **(c-conclusion)** The author believes the people must have the courage to believe they are good and useful. You can change things if you have the confidence to think you can succeed. That is the

author's point. Gaining a victory (a) helps build confidence, but people can have courage even before they win. People will provide their own leaders (b) if they have the courage to believe they are good and useful. The people in Pike County did not have a national organization (c), but they still won their battle.

8. **(d-vocabulary)** The word "rural" means country. It does not mean city, desert, or seashore. The passage is about Appalachian people in East Kentucky. That area is far from the sea (b). It is not a city (a) or anywhere near a desert (c).

9. **(word puzzle)**

¹M	²I	N	I	N	G		³W	I	N
	N						O		
	J				⁴P	A	R	K	
⁵R	U	R	A	L			K		
	S				⁶P		⁷C		
⁸S	T	E	E	L	⁹O	E	O		
	I				W		A		
¹⁰C	H	A	N	G	E		L		
	E				R				

~~~~~~~~ *11* ~~~~~~~~~~~~~~~~~~~~~~~~~~~~~~~~~~~~~

1. **(b-supporting detail)** The Black people of Selma tried to march for their right to vote. You can find this in the second sentence of the first paragraph. Some people might also have wanted the things listed in the other answer choices. But according to the passage, these things were not the purpose of the Selma march.

2. **(c-vocabulary)** The word "wailing" most nearly means "weeping out loud." Look at the way the word is used. You are told that the people in the church felt beaten, like they are at their "own funeral." You are told that some were crying, or weeping. They did start speaking *(b)* and singing *(a)* out loud, but they did that later. Although they were in a church, they were not at a regular prayer service *(d)*, and the author does not say the people were praying.

3. **(a-inference)** You can infer that the people felt strong when they began to sing. The second paragraph tells you that, when they went into a church, they were depressed *(c)*, and too beaten even to be afraid *(d)*. Singing as a group made them feel strong enough to face everything. In the sixth, seventh, and eighth paragraphs we are told that singing had given the people spirit, and the feeling that they had won. But even though they felt stronger, they couldn't really be free *(b)* until they had actually gotten their rights.

4. **(c-vocabulary)** The word "dirge" most nearly means a "sad song." In the fourth paragraph, the author says the tune had a "funeral sound," and that it was slow and soft. The other answer choices do not fit the way the sound is described. The humming was soft, not sharp, and it was not a cry *(a)*. Prayers *(b)* and speeches *(d)* are spoken words, but humming is only the tune of a song.

5. **(b-supporting detail)** The whole nation knew what had happened at Selma because it was on television. In the ninth paragraph, you are told that the "television cameras had gotten the whole thing." The author is telling her story *(a)* long after the event. The passage does not tell you that the governor made a speech *(c)*. The first paragraph says that the police used brute force. You could infer that people were hurt *(d)*, but that was not the reason that the nation knew about Selma. The Selma march was important because of what the people were marching for, not just what had happened to the people marching.

6. **(b-inference)** When the author arrives at the church, she says that what she saw made her cry again. Reread the second paragraph. The author describes what she saw as people who were "too beaten" to have fear. She felt that they didn't care to "even try to win anything anymore." She is describing people who seem to have given up in defeat. She does say that the people "weren't afraid." But from what she goes on to say, you know that she isn't saying they have lost their fear *(a)*. Her point is that they are too dead in spirit to feel any fear. The people were crying *(c)*, but it is what the author saw that made her cry. The people and the author were tear gassed *(d)*. The author does say that her eyes were burning from the tear gas. But she had already stopped crying from that.

7. **(b-conclusion)** Reverend Reese says that the night in the Selma church was a turning point in the voting-rights drive in Selma because the people kept their dignity. You can figure this out by looking at the end of the last paragraph. A turning point is like a sign. It's something that you pass that means something. What the people of Selma had passed was a kind of test. Up until then, they had been non-violent. But they did not act toward the police as the police had acted toward them. After what happened it would have been natural for them to want to fight back with violence *(a)*, but they did not. They did sing together *(c)*, and this helped them to find strength. It helped them keep their dignity. But the singing itself was not the turning point. And it would still be some time before the Black people of Selma got to vote *(d)*.

8. **(d-detail)** According to the passage, Dr. King came back to Selma before the people got their right to vote. The ninth paragraph says that King was going to come to Selma the next day. That means the day after the meeting in the church. He was bringing help. This suggests that the people needed lots of help to get the right to vote. Look at the last paragraph. It's plain that the people planned to keep their drive going. But they had already marched *(a)*. They had already been seen on television *(b)*. People had seen what happened when they had tried to march. They had already been turned back by the police *(c)*. In the first paragraph you are told that their march was turned back "with brutal force." And in the second, Sheyann says her eyes were swollen from tear gas. In the last paragraph, she speaks of the "beating at the bridge." They had been beaten once, but Dr. King came back to Selma to help them win.

~~~~~~~~ *12* ~~~~~~

1. **(b-main idea)** The best title for the passage would be "Electricity: From Nature to You." The purpose of the passage is to describe how electricity begins in nature and reaches you in your home. The passage describes generators *(d)*, which produce electricity, and some safety tips are pointed out *(a)*. But these things are just details used to talk about the main idea. The passage does not discuss the uses of electrical energy *(c)*.

2. **(d-vocabulary)** An insulator doesn't carry electricity. You can find this in the fifth paragraph. There you are told that insulators are used

where electric wires meet the supporting poles. You are told that a material through which electricity cannot pass is needed to keep the electricity from traveling through the poles to the ground. Since insulators do not carry electricity, answer choice *(c)* is wrong. You are told that an insulator may break, but the passage does not say how often this happens. Thus, answer choices *(a)* and *(b)* are both wrong.

3. **(d-supporting detail)** The passage states in the second paragraph that electricity has no color, size, or weight. The other three statements are not true. The passage does not say that electricity has any temperature *(a)*. It also says that insulators <u>keep</u> electricity from passing through them *(b)*. It can pass only through a <u>broken</u> insulator. Steam is used to make electricity, not the other way around *(c)*.

4. **(b-conclusion)** The passage states that electricity is made from converting the energy found in natural fuels. Winds, tides, and sunlight *(d)* are called "possible" sources. However, the passage says energy from these sources is not available yet in the amounts we need. The passage describes heat from the earth *(a)* as another "possible" source. Magnetic fields *(c)* are used in generating power, but they are just one of many forces used in converting the energy stored in natural fuels.

5. **(b-supporting detail)** According to the passage and the drawing, the overhead cables running from a generating plant to a substation are carrying high-voltage electricity. Look at the fifth paragraph. There it says that the cables are "high-voltage" cables because they carry a great deal of electric current. They are not carrying current for your home *(a)*, or to a transformer *(c)* because the voltage is too high for those to handle. Low-voltage electricity is what flows from a transformer to your home *(d)*. Use the drawing to see that the power starts out as high voltage and is lowered by the substation first and then by the transformer. Then it enters your house.

6. **(c-inference)** You can infer that the author tells you not to touch something that's in contact with a downed power line because there may be no insulation. Go back to the sixth paragraph. It says that people near a downed power line are in danger of electric shock. It tells you not to touch or go near the line. In the fifth paragraph, you are told that insulators keep the electricity from traveling through the poles. If a line is down, it probably has no insulators on it. Without insulators, you would have nothing to keep the electricity away from you. It would go through you or anything else in contact with the line that was not insulated. The passage doesn't mention other lines falling *(a)* or a falling pole *(d)*. It doesn't say if a broken wire is dangerous or not *(b)*.

7. **(a-conclusion)** The seventh paragraph of the passage tells you that power is reduced, or lowered, before it is sent into your home. Meters are used to measure the amount of electricity you can use <u>after</u> it has come into your home *(b)*. The passage does not talk about the effect that overhead wires *(c)*, or protected equipment *(d)* have on the power that goes to your home.

8. **(d-vocabulary)** The word "converted" is closest in meaning to "changed." Look at the third paragraph. It says that natural fuels are converted, or <u>changed</u>, into electrical energy. The passage lists several fuels (such as oil) that have energy stored in them. When the oil is burned, the energy inside it is released. The energy changes its form. The energy that is released is used to generate electricity *(b)*, but the energy itself is not generated. It is the electricity. that is transmitted *(c)*, and nothing in the paragraph suggests the energy is united with anything *(a)*.

13

1. **(c-main idea)** The best title for the passage is "How to Prevent Food Poisoning." The passage is about preparing and storing food safely. It gives the symptoms of food poisoning *(d)*. It also compares those symptoms with flu symptoms *(b)*. But these symptoms are not the main subject of the passage. They are details used to support the main idea. The passage is about making safe lunches, not good ones *(a)*.

2. **(d-supporting detail)** According to the passage, you don't have to remember not to freeze chicken or meat sandwiches when you're preparing a bag lunch. In fact, in the sixth paragraph, the author says that freezing sandwiches is a good idea. Answer choice *(a)* can be found in the third paragraph, and *(b)* in the fourth. Answer choice *(d)* is in the fifth paragraph.

3. **(c-conclusion)** According to the passage, if you make a safe bag lunch, the person who eats the lunch will not get food poisoning. A safely prepared lunch will not keep you from getting the flu *(d)* or some other "bug" *(a)*. The lunch may or may not be big enough to keep the person who eats it from getting hungry *(b)*.

4. **(a-inference)** The author will probably agree with the statement that being careful can help you stay healthy. The author shows how you can prevent food poisoning, so he probably believes you can prevent

other illnesses, too. Everyone does not get food poisoning *(c)*. The passage says it is hard to tell the difference between flu and food poisoning symptoms, but it does not say these two illnesses have the same cause *(d)*. In the second paragraph the author says that the methods for packing a safe lunch are "simple," not hard *(b)*.

5. **(c-vocabulary)** The word "precautions" most nearly means "safety measures." The passage tells you about some things you can do to keep your family safe from food poisoning. The second paragraph says that there are a few key methods, or measures, you should use. This paragraph isn't about warnings *(a)* or danger signals *(b)*. The passage tells you how to pack and store food safely, not how to cook it *(d)*.

6. **(Word jumble)**

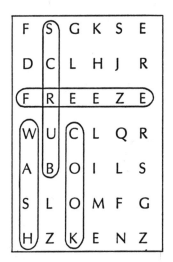

7. **(a-vocabulary)** The word "symptom" most nearly means "sign." Look at the way the word is used in the first paragraph. It is used to describe things like fever and cramps. These things are not diseases *(b)* or illnesses *(c)* themselves—they are small signs of a larger illness, like flu or food poisoning. These things do not cause food poisoning *(d)*, bacteria does.

8. **(b-inference)** You can infer that you should wear rubber gloves if you have cuts or sores because cuts and sores contain bacteria. Look at the fourth paragraph. It tells you to keep things clean and to use a fork, not your fingers, to make a sandwich. This helps stop the spread of bacteria. From this, you can guess that bacteria are the reason for covering up cuts and sores as well. The passage does not say that gloves will protect <u>you</u> from infection *(a)*. The point is that they protect others. Gloves may or may not be easier to clean than your hands *(c)*. Nothing is said about pain in the passage *(d)*.

~~~~~~~~~ *14* ~~~~~~

1. **(c-main idea)**   Men should spend time with their children because children need fathers as much as mothers. In the second paragraph, you are told that studies have found that fathers are important to the growth of a whole human being. The fourth paragraph says that a father is not just a "mother's helper." This means answer choice *(b)* is wrong. The rest of the passage tells you how men can get more involved with their children. Children do love to play with their fathers *(a)*, but playing with children is only one part of being a good father. The fifth paragraph tells you that a father should not try to fit into a mold *(d)*, and the eighth paragraph goes on to say that fathering "comes in many styles."

2. **(a-supporting detail)**   The passage states that you can be a good father and never bathe or dress an infant. The author points out some ways to prepare for being a father. She includes talking to other men *(b)*, thinking about fatherhood *(c)*, and reading books and magazines *(d)*.

3. **(d-conclusion)**   The passage states that if a new father shares his experiences with other fathers, his joy will grow. The last paragraph tells you this. The author doesn't mention how his friends *(a)* or his baby *(b)* will feel if he does this. The passage says that his problems will shrink, not his fears *(c)*.

4. **(a-conclusion)**   According to the passage, fathers spent less time with their children years ago than they do today because they had to work longer hours. You can find this in the fourth paragraph. The author says that in her grandfather's day, men worked very long hours, and that they hardly ever saw their children awake. She does not say that they were not interested in fathering *(b)*, or that they didn't love their families *(c)*. She does not say that they were uncomfortable about being fathers *(d)*.

5. **(d-inference)**   The passage states that the one essential ingredient in fathering is loving. You can find this in the eighth paragraph. There, "loving" is described as giving to and giving up for someone else's welfare. The other choices are all things that are part of fathering. But the author does not say that these are the most important parts of good fathering.

6. **(b-supporting detail)**   The passage does not state that men today help with the delivery of the baby. You are told that men often attend classes *(a)*, stay in the labor room *(d)*, and care for the new baby at home *(c)*. The passage tells you that men may be present during the

birth. This does not mean that they actually help the doctor deliver the baby.

7. **(c-style/tone)**   The author's attitude is best described as encouraging. She is trying to encourage men to prepare for fatherhood. She wants them to look forward to caring for their babies. She gives many suggestions, and writes about the joys fathers will experience. She is not worried about fathers *(a)*, and there is nothing amusing in the passage *(b)*. She is very careful to be fair to men and women both *(d)*.

8. **(d-vocabulary)**   "Prenatal" means before birth. The passage tells you that men who are preparing for fatherhood attend prenatal classes with the mother-to-be. This helps you to understand that these men are not yet fathers, because the women are not yet mothers when the classes are held. The classes are given before the birth of the baby. Parent training *(a)* is what might go on at a prenatal class. Child care *(b)* and childbirth *(c)* are some things that might be taught in such classes.

⋙⋙⋙⋙ *15* ⋙⋙⋙⋙⋙⋙⋙⋙⋙⋙⋙⋙⋙⋙⋙⋙⋙⋙⋙⋙⋙⋙⋙⋙

1. **(d-main idea)**   The best title for this passage would be "A Working Woman Demands Her Rights." The main point of the passage is how the author lost her job because she was pregnant. The passage also tells you how she fought for her right to get unemployment benefits. Answer choices *(a)* and *(b)* are just two things that the author tried to do to help herself. Answer choice *(c)* is too general because it doesn't mention the author's specific problems.

2. **(a-inference)**   The author thought she would keep her job because her old boss told her not to worry. The author says that she believed her boss. Answer choices *(b)*, *(c)*, and *(d)* are details stated directly in the passage. They are true, but they did not have any effect on the author getting her job back.

3. **(c-supporting detail)**   When the author left her job, she received a check for less than $200. The author says she was given a baby present of $200, <u>but</u> taxes were taken out of this sum. Because of this, the check had to be for less than $200, so *(a)* is wrong. The author applied for, and got, unemployment benefits, but she didn't apply for any other kind of aid *(c)*. She was told she would have to fill out an application if she wanted to return, but she was not given one when she left *(d)*.

4. **(d-supporting detail)** According to the passage, when the author knew she was pregnant, she told her old boss first because her old boss was a woman. In the first paragraph the author says that her new boss was a man, so she went to her old boss, a woman. She doesn't say that she didn't like her new job (b), or that her new boss didn't like her (d). She was not thinking about maternity leave at that time (a).

5. **(b-supporting detail)** The author did not want to leave her job when she was seven months pregnant because she couldn't afford to. In the third paragraph, she says that it was hard for her to leave her job because she really needed the money. She couldn't afford to stop working. The passage does not tell you whether the author liked her job (a) or her boss (d). The author does not talk about staying at home instead of working (c).

6. **(d-conclusion)** You can conclude that the author waited a month before going to the unemployment office because she did not think she could get unemployment benefits. The company said the author had quit her job. If you quit your job, you cannot get unemployment benefits. The company forced the author to quit because she was pregnant, so she was covered by unemployment. But she believed them when they told her she could not get any benefits. She was having her first baby, but she was able to go to the unemployment office (a). The author does say that she needs money (b). She was forced to quit—she wasn't fired from her job (c).

7. **(a-inference)** You can infer that the author was not the only person with this kind of problem because other pregnant women at the company also lost their jobs. In the third paragraph, she says that after she left, other pregnant women at the company were also "let go." This means they lost their jobs. The unemployment supervisor talked only about the author's case (d), and there is no mention of other mothers at the unemployment office (b). The author's husband tells her it's legal for her to collect unemployment benefits, not for pregnant women to be fired (c).

16

1. **(c-vocabulary)** As a "maintenance man" the author was supposed to repair machinery. You can find this out from the first paragraph. When he was hired by the lumber company, the author told his boss

that he knew how to take care of the equipment. He also says that he didn't really know anything about machinery. But this is the job they gave him. He did not have to run the machinery *(b)*, or guard it *(a)*. He learned how to weld *(d)* while he was at the lumber yard, but that wasn't his job.

2. **(d-conclusion)** According to the information in the passage, the author's main concern is finding a well-paying job. You can figure this out by reading the first paragraph. At the end of the paragraph, the author says he watched the welder because he knew that welders earned good salaries. This is why the author asked the welder to teach him to weld. He doesn't give any other reason for learning to weld other than the money. Later in the passage the author says that he left his job to work at the steel company. He did this because the pay was better there. The other answers are not supported by information in the passage. In the first paragraph the author says that he didn't work much on the machinery and he never says he ran the equipment *(c)*. And he left the lumber company as soon as he could *(b)*. He only goes to West Virginia *(a)* every once in a while, and then comes back, so you can infer that he likes working where he is now.

3. **(d-supporting detail)** When the author's skills as a welder improved, he got a better-paying job with a steel company. Read the sixth paragraph. After four or five months, the author became an excellent welder. He then left his job and went to work at the steel company. His new job payed $7.02 an hour. The author is no longer working for a lumber company, answer choices *(a)* and *(c)*. He does not work in West Virginia *(b)*. He lives there for part of the year.

4. **(c-inference)** The author would probably agree that federal jobs are the best because they pay so well. He earns $7.02 an hour on federal jobs at the steel company. This figure is repeated twice in the sixth paragraph. He's proud of the money he makes. This shows that the author thinks it is a high hourly wage. The author does not talk about how hard these jobs are *(a)*. He never says they are the easiest to be fired from *(b)*. The size of the government buildings is never mentioned in this passage *(d)*.

5. **(c-conclusion)** From the information in this passage you can conclude that the author wants to make good money, but he doesn't want to give up his whole life to get it. He enjoys earning a high salary working on federal jobs. However, he only works part of the year. He enjoys taking time off from work even though he's not earning any money when he does. The other answer choices are not supported by information in the passage. One of his fellow workers taught him how to weld, so they must have gotten along. He never

says that he doesn't like the people he works with *(a)*. He seems satisfied to remain a welder *(b)*. He tells an employer that he had his own welding truck *(d)*, but he just says that to get a job. There is no information in this passage to show that the author would like to own his own business.

6. **(c-style/tone)**   When the author talks about his job experiences, his tone is proud. In this passage, the author tells you how he came to a new place when he was 17 years old. He hadn't finished high school. But he beat the odds, he knows it, and he's proud of himself. He has learned a trade and made a good life for himself that he's happy with. And he did it on his own. He has a right to be proud of this kind of success. The other answers don't really fit. He is happy, but he's not joking *(a)*. Some people might think he was sneaky *(b)* because he lied to get ahead, but he is not trying to hide what he did. He plainly thinks he did what he had to do. He is excited, not bored *(d)*, with what he's been able to do.

7. **(b-main idea)**   The best title for this passage would be "Getting Ahead on the Job." This title tells you the most important idea in the passage. Throughout the passage, the author explains how he became a well-paid welder. First he lied about his job qualifications just so he could get a job. Then he spent all his time learning how to weld. He was able to find better and better jobs. None of the other answer choices covers the main idea of the passage. "Working for a Steel Company" *(a)* would be a good title for only the sixth paragraph. There, the author tells how he got his job at the steel company. "How to Become a Welder" *(c)* would be a good title for only the first paragraph. There, the author talks about how he learned to weld. "Finding Your First Job" *(d)* would be a good title for only the first paragraph. There he talks about getting his first job after he left high school.

17

1. **(d-main idea)**   The author feels that his job isn't the best, but it gives him the money to pay his bills. He tells you he can feed his family and pay for two cars. The author points out that some days are rough because of the younger workers. He says they often don't show up *(a)*. He talks about hours that are sometimes boring *(b)*, but says there

is a good union *(c)*. He mentions good points and bad points. These details help you figure out that the job is not the best and not the worst.

2. **(b-supporting detail)** The author describes the young generation as unsettled. In the second paragraph, he states that they just live from day to day, and do not have a routine *(c)*. This shows that they are not reliable *(a)*. The passage does not say they are proud *(d)*.

3. **(a-supporting detail)** The author tells you that he was grouchy because he got "stuck" when some of the other men didn't come to work. The author does not blame the foreman *(d)* or his bills *(c)* for his grouchy feelings. Being bored *(b)* is not the same as being grouchy, which means irritable.

4. **(c-supporting detail)** The author states in the second paragraph that when the younger workers settle down they will go to work every day. He says they will want to work when they settle down. They will get into a routine of work, as he has. He does not imply that people who settle down will like the company any more than they do now *(d)*. He says that workers who deserve respect *(a)* will get it, but he isn't talking about new workers. He talks about foremen who want to go to the top *(b)*, but not workers like himself.

5. **(b-conclusion)** You can conclude that the author has been working regularly. He states in the third paragraph that he has ". . . brought home a forty-hour paycheck for Lord knows how long." This tells you that he has been earning his full pay without any breaks. This could not have happened if he had been laid off *(a)* or out sick very often *(d)*. Nothing is said in the passage about the author getting a promotion *(c)*.

6. **(a-inference)** Most of the time the author is basically happy about his job. He tells you in the fifth paragraph that his ". . . day goes pretty good on the average." This implies that there is nothing wrong most of the time so he doesn't worry all the time *(c)*. The author writes about joking and teasing other workers. This tells you he has friends *(b)*. When he writes about wanting "quittin' time," he means he wants the day to end. It doesn't mean he wants to quit his job *(d)*.

7. **(d-conclusion)** The author feels that your attitude can most influence the way you do your job. He says in the third paragraph that a lot of your work is in your mind. He feels it would be harder for him if he hated the company *(b)*. His family *(a)* and his expenses *(c)* are the reasons he works. But he says he doesn't let other worries affect his work. He tells you that he can change his feelings about going to work even if he didn't feel like going at first.

8. **(d-conclusion)** The author seems to feel that his retirement is likely to be peaceful. In the last paragraph, he describes a little garden down South. He says that all he'll do is watch the sun come up and go down. He writes of fishing and hunting. These are peaceful scenes and they tell you how the author imagines his retirement will be. He likes these things, so he won't be bored (c). He has his family, so he won't be lonely (a). The life he describes clearly doesn't sound very difficult (b).

9. **(a-vocabulary)** The phrase "agreed upon" best expresses the meaning of "negotiated." In the seventh paragraph, the union and the company are said to have negotiated. The union protects the author, and he's happy with how things have worked out. You can figure out that the union and the company agreed on matters that were good for the workers. They may have built up (b) and argued over (d) benefits, but these things are just part of the long process of making an agreement. Management does not "give out" (c) things to the workers. The author's bosses have agreed to things the union wants in a process of give and take.

~~~~~~~~ *18* ~~~~~~~~~~~~~~~~~~~~~~~~~~~~~~~~~~~~~~~

1. **(a-main idea)** By "get their heads together" about housework, the author means that the women's rights groups had to change their attitudes about what housework means. Look at the first sentence. It says that these women believed their own view of housework was the only meaning it could have. You can see that the author felt these women had to change their thinking about the meaning of housework. She felt they had to do a lot more than just listen to the opinions of household workers (b). The author is not talking about the rights of household workers in the first paragraph (c). She never says whether household workers were or were not included in women's rights organizations (d).

2. **(c-inference)** The author thinks of herself and the other household workers as professionals because they are experienced. They are well paid for their experience. Look at the third paragraph. There the author tells of the money they earn and the skills they have gotten from experience. They think of themselves as professionals. The other answer choices are not good reasons for this. The workers want

respect because they are good at their jobs. But respect alone cannot make a person a professional *(a)*. Just because a group has a name doesn't make the members good at what they do *(b)*. The author clearly says that household work should not be thought of as a dirty job *(d)*.

3. **(b-main idea)** You can conclude that the <u>main</u> thing the household workers took pride in was the work they do. Read the third paragraph. The author's way of describing her work shows you that she and the other workers felt pride in their jobs. The workers' feelings about the author's speed *(a)* are never discussed. The workers are proud of the money they make *(c)* but this is a detail of their jobs. The group's attitude *(d)* is a good one, but it is a result of the pride they take in their work, not the reason for their pride.

4. **(c-conclusion)** You can conclude that the guests wanted to leave because the household workers were doing housework. In the first paragraph you find out that the guests had their own view of housework. They were upset when they came to the party and saw that "maids" were waiting on them. The workers are experienced and know their jobs, so it is unlikely they were spilling things *(b)*. The passage says that they were well paid, but there is nothing in the passage about the guests being upset about the fee *(a)*, or about the workers forming a group *(c)*.

5. **(d-vocabulary)** The "feminist" women at the party were most concerned with women's rights. In the first paragraph, the author describes the people at the party as belonging to women's rights groups. She says that they didn't understand her attitude about the meaning of housework *(c)*. In the next paragraph she says that the feminist women "couldn't deal with" the workers at the party, so the guests could not have been very concerned with the workers' rights *(b)*. The party itself *(a)* was probably of least concern for everyone there.

6. **(b-conclusion)** The main reason the author wore a uniform was that the uniform let people know who she was. In the fourth paragraph, she says that her uniform is the clothing of her profession. She compares it to a doctor wearing a white coat. She tells you that if a doctor is not wearing a white coat, she feels uncomfortable. Without a uniform, the doctor doesn't look like a doctor. The uniform lets her know the profession of the wearer. She does not say that she feels like a doctor *(a)*. The passage does not say how much a uniform costs *(c)*. The author does say that someone at the party might spill something on her, but she doesn't say this has happened before *(d)*.

19

1. **(d-main idea)**   The best title for the passage would be "A Woman's Apprenticeship." There is nothing in the passage to say that the author took a man's job away *(b)*. The author does talk about prejudice she has felt *(a)* and her experience with the union *(c)*, but she is only talking in the passage about how these things affected her personally. She is not talking about women generally. These titles would be good titles for a general passage about either subject.

2. **(c-vocabulary)**   The word "credibility" most nearly means "able to be believed." The whole passage is about the author's struggle to gain the respect of the men she works with, and the people she works for. She wants them to believe that she can do the work. In the second paragraph, she is talking about the attitudes of the men in her junior college class. She says that some people may still think she is a "freak," but that she knows more than most of the men. She has a better job. This gives her their respect. At the end of the fifth paragraph, she says that the apprenticeship papers give her credibility. The papers prove that she knows her job. This proof will make others believe her when she says she is a good mechanic. No paper can prove a person is able to be honest *(a)* or strong *(d)*. She is being taught *(b)*, but what she learns won't mean anything if people don't believe her.

3. **(d-inference)**   You can infer that the author feels unhappy about going to college because she already knows the things the college is teaching. In the first paragraph, the author says that she has already been to the same school, years before. In the second paragraph, she says that she's not learning anything and that she knows more than most of the men in her class. Answer choices *(a)* and *(b)* are the reasons she is staying in school. She does not say she would like school if it were a famous college *(c)*.

4. **(b-conclusion)**   You can conclude the author means that she can't really change men's ideas about women. She says that even though she is an exception, most of the men think women are "subhuman." She is saying that while she has their respect as an individual, she hasn't changed the men's basic attitudes. She may not like everything the union does *(a)*, but nothing in the passage says she is trying to change it. She isn't really afraid of being an exception *(c)*, and there's nothing in the passage that says that she is really worried about being liked by the men she works with *(d)*.

5. **(a-supporting detail)** According to the information in the passage, the author is working at a dealership. You can find this information in the first sentence. She is going to college *(d)*, but is not working there. It is another woman who works at the parts counter *(c)*. She says that some of the men in the class work in gas stations *(b)*, but she does not.

6. **(c-conclusion)** The author feels she needs to be in an apprenticeship program because she wants to be able to work anywhere she wants. In the fifth paragraph, she says that a man could probably get a good job anywhere he wants without going through an apprenticeship program. But she believes she couldn't do the same thing without her papers because she's a woman. She might want to do the things listed in answer choices *(a)*, *(b)*, and *(d)*, but they are not mentioned in the passage.

7. **(b-conclusion)** The author resents being given a four-year apprenticeship because she thinks she should get credit for her experience. You can find this information in the fifth paragraph. She thinks her experience should get her a two- or three-year apprenticeship instead. Answer choices *(a)*, *(c)*, and *(d)* may be true statements, but they do not explain her feeling about the length of her apprenticeship.

8. **(d-vocabulary)** As it is used in the passage, the word "journey" means the rank above apprentice. In the fifth paragraph, the author says that a man with a bunch of tools could convince a boss he was working at "journey level." Her point is that if he had a lot of tools, people would believe he probably had lots of experience—more than an apprentice. In the last paragraph, she talks about the parts technician who has just gotten her "journey papers." This sounds like she has gotten a promotion. "Journey" <u>does</u> mean "taking a trip" *(a)*, but not as it's used in this passage. There is nothing in the passage that supports *(b)*, and nothing that says only parts technicians can have this rank *(c)*.

20

1. **(b-vocabulary)** The word "routine" could be used in place of "ritual." You can figure this out from the context. The author is talking about the things that Chris and Kate did together every night before they went to bed. The main point of the paragraph is that they always did the same things again and again—their actions were "routine." "Different" (a) and "variety" (d) are the opposites of "routine." A prayer (c) can be called a ritual, but it doesn't fit the context here—the author does not say if Kate and Chris prayed.

2. **(b-main idea)** "The Problem With Nursing Homes" could not be used as a title for this passage. This title would be good for a newspaper story about the many problems people may have with nursing homes. Also, it is not about the problems of all nursing homes. It's about the love Kate and Chris had for each other in their last years together. The other titles all deal with Kate and Chris and their problems.

3. **(d-supporting detail)** After Chris tucked Kate in bed and turned off her light, he kissed her. You can find this information in the seventh paragraph. Kate and Chris then said "Goodnight" to each other, so he did not read (a) or put on his pajamas (b). The author says that she was in the hall, so Chris couldn't be talking to her (d).

4. **(c-vocabulary)** The word "policies" most nearly means "rules." The author is talking about the fact that nursing homes don't allow couples to sleep in the same bed. This is a rule. The author says she thinks it's a foolish rule. The rule may have started out as an idea (b), but now it is a fact. The word "manners" (a) means the way people act, and "feelings" (d) means emotions.

5. **(d-inference)** The author thinks that nursing homes should have double beds because married couples are used to sleeping together. In the sixth paragraph, the author wonders why older couples must sleep in separate beds when they have slept together all their lives. Kate and Chris did not complain about their beds (b), and nothing is said about how comfortable the beds are (c). Since Kate and Chris are in separate beds, it does not matter how far apart they are (a).

6. **(d-inference)** You can infer that after Chris died, bedtime was the hardest time for Kate because she felt most alone then. Kate was used to having Chris tuck her in and kiss her goodnight. When he died she had no one to kiss her goodnight. That was when she needed Chris the most. There is nothing in the passage that says

Kate was afraid of the dark *(a)*, wanted more pills *(c)*, or couldn't sleep in the single bed.

7. **(b-inference)** You can infer that the author kissed Kate goodnight because it would help Kate sleep. The author says that after Chris died, Kate would lie awake all night. Chris had always kissed her goodnight, and Kate had slept well. Kate hadn't asked the author to do anything *(a)*, and it wasn't really the author's job to kiss the patients goodnight *(c)*. Kate didn't start crying until after the author had kissed her *(d)*.

8. **(b-inference)** You can infer that the scrapbook held pictures of Chris and Kate through the years together. In the first paragraph, the author says the book held pictures of Chris and Kate through the passing seasons. In the next paragraph, it says that the old couple smiled "at the memories of the years," held forever in the scrapbooks. There is no mention of their children *(a)* or any single day *(d)*. The pictures were of the past, not the present in the nursing home *(c)*.

9. **(Word jumble)**

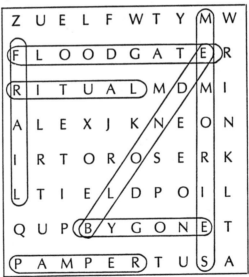

10. **(b-supporting detail)** Chris was not always lonely. All through the author's description of their life together, the most important fact is that they kept each other company. It is clear that they loved each other *(a)*, and in the fourth paragraph the author says that "Chris was the strong one, and Kate was dependent on him" *(d)*. The first paragraph says that Chris was "tall, blond, and handsome," and that Kate was "pretty" and "dark-haired" in their old photos *(b)*. But Chris could never be lonely when he had Kate.

21

1. **(a-main idea)** The best title for this passage would be "My Thoughts on American Street Names." The passage is about the author's personal opinions of American street names. The author does not talk about how to change our street names *(b)*, or about great English street names *(d)*, even though the author mentions some of them. The passage does list the most popular American street names *(c)*. But the author only does this so he can tell you what he thinks of them.

2. **(c-vocabulary)** "Originality" is closest in meaning to the word "creativity." Look at the second paragraph. The author compares American street names to street names in other countries. He calls those names "great." To him, they sound interesting and unusual. He thinks our street names sound plain and dull. In the third paragraph, he uses the fact that some of our most important streets have numbers for names as an example. Numbers are <u>not</u> original. The author thinks that if we took the trouble to think and be creative, we could come up with better names for our streets. The other answers don't fit the context. The author isn't talking about how rich *(a)* the people who live on a street are, or how great *(b)* a street is. He talks about both important and ordinary streets. And he does not say that just being foreign *(d)* makes a street name better.

3. **(1-b, 2-e, 3-d, 4-c, 5-a-supporting detail)** In the third and fourth paragraphs we read that the most common street names are: first, Park; second, Washington; third, Maple; fourth, Oak; and fifth, Lincoln. The author gives them to us in reverse order. We read about the fifth most common street name first. Then comes the fourth most common. This goes on until he gets to the "winner," which is Park.

4. **(d-supporting detail)** The author's information about common American street names came from the postal service. You can find this at the end of the fourth paragraph. He does not say he traveled for himself to check up on street names *(b)*. He did not get the information from a housing development office *(a)* or from a national newspaper survey *(c)*.

5. **(c-conclusion)** According to this passage, when a developer calls an area by a name other than "street," he hopes that people will pay more for the houses. The ninth paragraph says that the developer can try to get more money for a house on a street with a fancy name. It says the developer tries to add "class" in this way. Calling an area "Lane" instead of "Street" will not make the people who

buy the houses "classy" *(a)*. The passage does not say that the area will become a landmark because of its name *(b)*, or that the developer cares if it does or not. When the author uses the expression "ticky-tack," he means that the houses are not well built. He does not say that the developer is trying to fool the buyers with a name *(d)*. The developer is just using the name to advertise the houses.

6. **(Word jumble)**

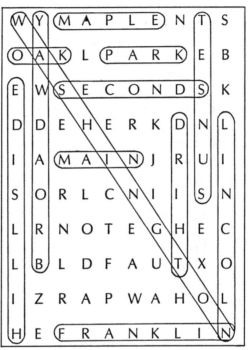

7. **(c-supporting detail)** According to the author, calling a street Wolf Lane doesn't make much sense because there are no wolves there now. The author says that, if a street is named Wolf Lane now, it's probably been a hundred years since anyone saw a wolf there. You can find this in seventh paragraph. He uses Wolf Lane as one example of street names that don't make sense because they suggest something about the street that isn't true. He does not tell you anything about the names of the families who live there *(a)*. Nothing is said about whether there ever were *(b)* or weren't *(d)* wolves in the area. He is saying that the people who name streets name them for reasons of their own. These reasons don't have to be logical or really make sense.

8. **(b-style/tone)** The author's attitude toward American street names is this passage is best described as joking. The author says that many of our great streets don't even have names: They just have numbers. In the third paragraph he says our numbered streets are dull. As an

124

example he mentions Forty-second Street. He adds, "Would you write a song about a street with a name like that?" But there is a popular song about New York's Forty-second Street. The author is also trying to be funny with his description of the way housing developers name streets. When the author tells you about the most popular American street names, he says he'll list them backward, "like a Miss America contest." Of course, there is no contest here. The author is just making a big deal about some facts he got from the postal service. But even though he is being critical about American street names, he is being light about it. The author isn't being nasty (a) or angry (c). He is criticizing the names of American streets and praising the street names in foreign countries. So he could not really be called patriotic in this passage (d).

9. **(b-conclusion)** The author of this passage would most likely agree that Americans should give more thought to naming their streets. The second paragraph says that we Americans haven't shown much originality in naming our streets. He says many of them are just named after trees or former Presidents. Many have only numbers for names. Land developers pick cute street names to sell houses. Although he doesn't like some street names, he doesn't suggest that Americans should be unhappy with them (a). He might like to see some streets get new names, but he doesn't suggest that Americans should run out and start renaming their streets right away (c). He likes some English street names, but he does not say that Americans should just copy the English. (d).

22

1. **(c-main idea)** The main purpose of the passage is to alert people against different kinds of frauds and swindles. The passage goes on to describe several kinds of things to beware of. The other answer choices are some of these things. They are details from the passage. The passage shows how we might be fooled by junk mail (a), door-to-door sellers (b), and crooked contracts (d).

2. **(d-supporting detail)** The passage lists all of the answer choices as examples of possible fraud EXCEPT free legal aid. The second and third paragraphs tell you that the legal aid society in your area can give you free legal advice. They can help you in dealing with

people who might be trying to cheat you. So, not everything that's free of charge is a gimmick. The third paragraph warns you about "free" offers at the door (a), and the second tells you to beware of offers of "easy" money that come in the mail (b). The fifth paragraph tells you not to be fooled by "low" monthly payments (c).

3. **(b-supporting detail)** According to the passage, mortgaging your house will not make a contract safe to sign. You can mortgage your home if you need to borrow a large amount of money. You usually get a mortgage from a bank or a finance company, and these places are watched by the government. This keeps them honest. But just because you mortgage your home to an honest bank doesn't mean you'll get what you want when you spend the money. The eighth paragraph warns you against mortgaging your house just for a few repairs because you don't understand the contract. It also tells you to check with the Better Business Bureau (c). The fourth paragraph tells you to check with a lawyer (a). The last suggests you talk to a bank officer (d).

4. **(c-inference)** If a seller objects to being checked out, you can infer that the seller is probably trying to cheat you. Look at the ninth paragraph. It says that the only sellers that will object to this are the ones trying to take advantage of you. You can infer that they are trying to hide something from you. Many sellers do try to pressure you to buy (a), but this doesn't mean they will object to being checked out—unless they are trying to cheat you as well. Not all people selling land are dishonest (b). The third paragraph tells you to watch out for people offering "free" gifts (d). It does not say they will always object to being checked out.

5. **(a-conclusion)** The author would probably agree that bargains can sometimes be expensive. The seventh paragraph states that a bargain is not a bargain if it won't help you the way it is supposed to. Also, in the first paragraph, you are warned against "bargain" plots of land. And, in the sixth paragraph, you are warned against "bargain-priced" health products. The author does not say that all salespeople are dishonest (b) or that all land in Florida isn't a bargain (c). He tells you in the fifth paragraph that "low" monthly payments may be costly to you (d).

6. **(b-inference)** The passage advises that buyers CANNOT be too suspicious. When the authors suggests that a buyer check out a seller, he is implying that it is your right to be suspicious of an offer. The passage points out ways to protect yourself from fraud (a). It does say that the post office can help you (d), and there are many ways a buyer can make sure a bargain is really a bargain (b).

7. **(d-inference)** The passage refers to different agencies that can help you to check on a seller. The passage doesn't answer the other questions. Those are the kind of questions you could ask of the "helpers" mentioned in the passage. Agencies like the Better Business Bureau, lawyers and the legal aid society, the police, the post office, and community action centers are pointed out as places to go for help in getting answers to your questions about sellers who have cheated you.

8. **(c-vocabulary)** "Junk" mail could be called "trash" mail. The passage describes how junk mail offers you things that are "free" or "bargains" that you might not want or care about. Things that you don't want are trash. Some junk mail is dishonest *(b)*, ugly *(a)*, or offers things with cheap prices *(d)*, but most is simply mail you do not need.

9. **(c-inference)** According to the passage, interest charges may seem to be too much. The author tells you in the fifth paragraph to check with a bank or a community action center if you think this is so. This paragraph also tells you that interest payments are <u>extra</u> charges. They are <u>one</u> kind of extra charge *(b)*. This tells you they are not the actual price of the item *(a)*. It also tells you that they are not subtracted from the price *(d)*.

10. **(Word problem)**

   1. (B)ETTER BUSINESS BUREAU
   2. H(E)ALTH CLINIC
   3. LA(W)YER
   4. LEG(A)L AID
   5. MAYO(R)
   6. POLIC(E)

   The hidden message is: BEWARE!

23

1. **(b-main idea)** The author's main goal after her first job here was to live independently. In the third paragraph she says that working here would be her "living joy" because she could express herself. She tells you she was so happy when she thought she would have her own money at last. Then, she feels she could be as free as a

real American. Learning English *(a)*, buying clothes *(b)*, and earning money *(c)* would make her more like other Americans. But these things were only <u>part</u> of her goal. These things would help her express herself with her work and life.

2. **(d-supporting detail)**   The author tells you that her employers were well-dressed. She says this in the fifth paragraph. She tells you they were ashamed of their mother tongue, and that they came from the same village the author came from. This was in Russia. Since they were ashamed of the Russian language, they wouldn't speak it very often *(b)*. Since the employers came from the same village as the author, they could not have been born in America *(a)*. The size of their house *(c)* is not mentioned.

3. **(s-supporting detail)**   The passage does not say that the author ironed clothes. It does say in the eleventh paragraph that she prepared breakfast *(b)*. The sixth paragraph tells you that she scrubbed floors *(c)* and scoured pots *(d)*.

4. **(b-conclusion)**   The author was often hungry in Russia. In the third paragraph, she writes about the "dead drudgery" for bread in Russia. She uses the phrase "slave of the belly." This tells you that there was not enough food. It does not mean she was really a slave *(a)*. The author tells you that work was denied her in Russia so she was not a worker *(c)*. She writes that working here would be a way to express herself. This does not mean she was rich *(d)* in Russia.

5. **(b-conclusion)**   Getting paid depended on the author learning English. You can figure this out from the words of the employer: "Wait 'til you're worth any money. What use are you without knowing English?" The passage does not suggest that the employers expected the author to work harder *(a)*. She could not dress well unless she was paid *(c)*. They did not tell her to stay longer *(d)* in order to get paid.

6. **(a-vocabulary)**   The expression "mother tongue" means the language of her employers' homeland. The passage tells you the family was "Americanized." This means that they had become like Americans. You can conclude that they spoke English. This was the language of their new country *(c)*. They were ashamed of the language they had spoken in their village. The author tells you that the family came from the same village as she. The author doesn't mention anyone's mother *(b)* or any other servants *(d)*.

7. **(c-inference)**   The author states that she wanted to look like an American. This tells you that she wanted to look like everyone else. She writes that she needed clothes to forget that she was a stranger and looked like an immigrant. She says she wanted money in her

hands to buy the clothes. The clothes were not for her job *(d)*. She doesn't say she wanted to look rich *(b)*. She just wanted to look like an American. She did not want to forget who she was *(a)*.

8. **(d-conclusion)** The author felt that Americans did not understand her. Americans did not give her "a smile of understanding" because she could not speak English. She had a job, so she could not feel they would not hire her *(b)*. The passage does not say anyone disliked the author *(a)* or did not want her here *(c)*.

9. **(b-inference)** The author was very upset. Look at the last paragraph. She tells you that she was so choked that she could not speak. By the words, "The tears went dry in my throat," you can infer that she was about to cry. The passage does not give you any reason to believe that the author was guilty *(a)*, annoyed *(d)*, or embarrassed *(c)*.

10. **(a-vocabulary)** The word "dead" is closest in meaning to the word "sterile." In the second paragraph, the author calls America the "land of <u>living</u> hope." In the next paragraph, she compares the "golden land of opportunity" to her village. She calls her village "sterile," and all the words she uses to describe America are words of life and freedom. From this you can conclude that she was happy to be here because America was alive and hopeful, and that her village was dead. She doesn't say that her village was sad *(b)* or dirty *(c)*. She does say she was often hungry *(d)* in her village, but this word doesn't fit the context of the third paragraph.

11. **(d-inference)** You can infer that, for the author, learning English was like a discovery. Look at the seventh paragraph. There the author tells you how excited she was about learning English. She asked all kinds of people to help her learn. She says that learning the language of Americans made her see things through "American eyes." And in the last sentence, she says she felt like Columbus, the discoverer of the New World. She knows that learning English will help her in her job, but it is not really a job by itself *(a)*. She doesn't say she was doing it for anyone but herself, so learning English was not a service *(b)*. It was not a painful experience *(c)*; she enjoyed learning her new language.

12. **(s-style/tone)** The author felt that her employers were unfair. Her employers had told her she was not worth anything without knowing English, yet she had worked very hard for them. You can conclude that she felt it was very unfair for her not to get any money for all the work she did. The passage does not suggest that the employers were forgetful *(c)* or dissatisfied *(d)* with the author's work. Her

employers may have been cheap *(b)*, but that is not what the author is talking about in the passage.

13. **(d-vocabulary)** In this passage, the word "dumb" in the first sentence means "silent." The author uses the word "voiceless" to describe her situation in America. This is a poetic way of saying that she wanted to be heard. But since she did not know the language, she was silent, with no voice, because she could not speak English. She was not deaf *(b)*. You can tell she is not ignorant from the way she writes *(a)*. She isn't hopeless *(c)* at all. She will try to learn English.

24

1. **(d-supporting detail)** The author called her son "the king of the rats" because he seemed to be hurting Andy. Look at the twelfth paragraph. At the start, she says that she didn't know for sure what David had really done. What she <u>thought</u> he had done was hurt Andy. Later in the paragraph you are told that Andy was pleading for David to "STOP!" and that he sounded like he was being strangled. It was Billy who wouldn't wear his boots *(a)* and screamed "I hate you!" at Helen *(b)*. Helen is the one who hit Billy on the ear *(c)*.

2. **(a-main idea)** The women are talking about what happens when they get angry with their children. First Helen describes her behavior when she got angry with her son Billy. Then the author tells Helen about what happened when she got angry with her son David. The passage doesn't say that Helen and the author were tired of their children *(b)* or unhappy with their children's school work *(c)*. The two mothers are upset because of what happened when they got angry with their sons. They are worried because they are trying to be good parents, so they are not careless parents *(d)*.

3. **(c-supporting detail)** Helen got angry at her son because he refused to wear his boots. She started to get angry when she saw he was wearing only his sneakers *(b)*, but she says she was able to control herself. He had been sick all week *(a)* but this is not what she got angry about. She was worried that he would get sick again if he just wore sneakers. He screamed at her <u>after</u> she showed her

anger by scolding him and throwing the boots at him. This is not what made her angry *(d)*.

4. **(c-inference)**   The author's reason for not telling Helen her own story right away was that she was too ashamed to tell her. She says that something held her back from telling Helen what had happened. Then Helen talks about her own experiences some more. After hearing about Helen's anger, the author feels that Helen will understand. She may also feel that someone else has the same problem. The author and Helen are friends. The author isn't afraid of Helen's reaction *(a)*. The author never talks about wanting to forget the fight *(b)*. She is not still angry when she speaks to Helen *(d)*. She is ashamed and upset at what had happened.

5. **(a-supporting detail)**   When the author got angry she didn't ask her sons what they were doing because she wanted them to work it out by themselves. You can find this in the twelfth paragraph. She says she didn't even know what David did to Andy. She heard some sounds from the boys' room which might have been David hurting Andy, but they might have been just playing. She doesn't say she was trying not to get angry *(b)*. She told her friend Helen about it afterward, but she doesn't say she wanted to talk to Helen first *(c)*. She did tell Helen she had read about an experiment *(d)*, but that experiment was about rats and monkeys, not human beings.

6. **(b-vocabulary)**   The word "happily" best expresses the meaning of the word "gleefully." Even if Andy wasn't having a good time, David seemed to be. David was a child, but he wasn't acting in a way most people would think of as "childish" *(a)*. He was being violent with Andy, but it's hard to think of a laugh itself as "violent" *(c)*. "Hopeful" *(d)* doesn't fit the context of the paragraph.

7. **(d-style/tone)**   Helen probably felt relieved after hearing the author's story. She says that she feels better knowing that she isn't the only person to get mad. In the eleventh paragraph she tells the author, "I feel better already." She was no longer angry *(a)*, and she wasn't jealous of the author *(c)*. The ending of the passage is not very hopeful *(b)*.

8. **(b-inference)**   The purpose of the experiment was to find out what happened when rats and monkeys got angry. The paragraph tells you that the experiment was about rats and monkeys who had been angered. The scientists tried many things to frustrate the animals, and then watched what they did. The scientists already knew what happened when the animals scratched and bit each other *(a)*. Nothing is said about the animals hurting their babies *(c)*. They were frustrated and angry. They did not feel good *(d)*.

9. **(d-supporting detail)** In the experiment on anger described by the author, the animals seemed to feel good when they hurt each other. The author tells you that something in their bodies changed so that they actually felt good when they hurt each other. The things mentioned in the other answer choices did not happen in the experiment. It did not deal with mothers and their children *(a)* and *(b)*. The passage doesn't say the animals stopped biting and clawing each other *(c)*.

10. **(a-conclusion)** The author would probably agree that anger is something to learn how to handle. Although at first she did not want to talk about her own anger, she seems to be trying to understand it. She read about an experiment having to do with anger. She thinks about what she has read, and how it relates to her. Then she discusses it with her friend. She is bothered by her own behavior when she is angry. She may have been ashamed of her <u>behavior</u>, but not of her anger itself *(b)*. She knows her own anger got out of control this time. But she does not say anger should always be controlled *(c)*. And she seems to know that anger can sometimes be controlled, even though she and Helen, like other people, have trouble doing so. There is no information in the passage to tell you she thinks anger can never be controlled *(d)*.

25

1 **(c-main idea)** The purpose of the passage is to give drivers a review of some basic rules for safe driving. You can find this in the first paragraph. The rules for driving in every state *(a)* or in the driver's own state are not given *(d)*. For these things, the author suggests that drivers should consult their Driver's Manual or their state's traffic laws. The passage uses an imaginary trip as a way to review driving rules, but the purpose of the passage is not to give a road map of such a trip *(b)*.

2 **(b-vocabulary)** "Give" could best be used instead of "yield." The author says that you must "yield the right of way to pedestrians on the sidewalk. Then you must yield the right of way to cars on the street. . . ." When you yield you give the right of way. You are recognizing that the other person or car has the right to go before you do. Answer choices *(a)*, *(c)*, and *(d)* do not have this meaning.

3. **(a-supporting detail)** Your car has the right of way at an intersection without traffic lights or signs if it is to the right of another car. You can find this in the last sentences of the fifth paragraph. You do not have the right of way if your car is on the left *(b)*. Nothing is said in that paragraph about whether the car on the left has already crossed the intersection *(c)*. Nothing is said about a car coming in the opposite direction *(d)*.

4. **(c-conclusion)** When a car comes to an intersection controlled by a flashing red light, it must come to a full stop and then cross when the way is clear. You can find this in the sixth paragraph. A red light always means "full stop." It does not mean "slow down" *(b)*. The flashing light means that you can go again when the way is clear. A flashing red light will never change to yellow, so answer choices *(a)* and *(d)* are wrong.

5. **(a-NO; b-YES; c-YES; d-NO–supporting detail)** In the ninth paragraph the author tells you that a double solid line *(drawing a)* prohibits passing. This means that passing is not allowed. You are told that a solid line with a broken line on one side means that a car on the broken-line side may pass. This situation is shown in drawing *(c)*. You may pass here because your car is on the broken-line side. It is also shown in drawing *(d)*, but here you may not pass. Here, your car is on the solid-line side. You are also told that when there is a broken line, cars on either side of the line may pass. This is shown in drawing *(d)*.

6. **(d-vocabulary)** "Destination" means "last stop." In the last paragraph, you are told that when you reach your destination, the trip is over. You have come to the last stop, the end of your journey. Answer choices *(a)* and *(b)* <u>might</u> be your last stop, but they don't <u>have</u> to be. They may or may not be your destination. Answer choice *(c)* cannot be the last stop.

7. **(c-inference)** A man driving at 25 m.p.h. in a 45 m.p.h. zone is probably driving unsafely. Look at the fourth paragraph. The last sentence tells you to drive at a speed that is "reasonable." Unless it was raining, or the road was very bad, or the man's car was in trouble, it is not reasonable to be driving at 25 m.p.h. in a 45 m.p.h. zone. Driving too slowly, like driving too fast, can put you and other drivers in danger. It isn't safe to drive much more slowly than other drivers expect you to. The man may be trying to be careful *(a)*, but he's really not driving carefully. There is no way to know the driver's age *(b)*, or how long he's been driving *(d)*.

8. **(a-supporting detail)** According to the passage, when a traffic officer gives instructions, a driver must obey, even if it means going

through a red light. You can find this information in the next-to-last paragraph. The instructions of a traffic officer come before anything else. You may go through a red light if an officer tells you to. So answer choice (b) is not correct. Although you should always be aware of other vehicles, you should not look to see what other drivers are doing (c) or if an emergency vehicle is coming (d) before obeying the officer.

9. **(b-supporting detail)** In the eighth paragraph you can find that 55 miles per hour is the legal maximum speed in most states. Other speed limits may apply. But this is true only if they are posted on signs by the side of the road. Sixty miles per hour (a) is the old limit, but it was lowered to 55 in the 1970s. Thirty-five (c) is too low, and 65 (d) is too high.

10. **(d-supporting detail)** According to the passage you may <u>not</u> pass a school bus that has stopped for passengers. You can find this in the tenth paragraph. The eighth paragraph tells you to keep to the right lane except when something is blocking that lane (a). Nothing is said about passing a car on a city street (b). The ninth paragraph says that you may pass a vehicle going in the same direction (c) if the road markings allow you to.

11. **(Word problem)**
    ETRETS: STREETS
    AYHGIHW: HIGHWAY
    AIVDWREY: DRIVEWAY
    ICFRAFT ELCICR: TRAFFIC CIRCLE

READING SKILLS CHART

Passage Number	Finding the Main Idea	Finding Supporting Detail	Making Inferences	Understanding Vocabulary in Context	Drawing Conclusions	Recognizing Style & Tone	Word Problems, Jumbles & Puzzles	DISCUSSION: Thinking About What You Have Read
1	1, 2	4, 7	8	3, 6	5			9
2	1	2	3, 5	7	4, 6	8		9
3			1, 3	2	4		5	6
4	1	2	3, 6	5	4			7
5	8	1, 2	3	5, 7	4, 6			9
6	1	7	2, 6	4	3, 5	8	8	9, 10
7	1	2, 3	4	5	7	6	9	9
8	1	2, 3	4	8	5, 6, 7			
9	1	2, 3		6	4, 5			7
10	1	2, 3	5, 6	8	4, 7		9	10
11		1, 5, 8	3, 6	2, 4	7			9, 10
12	1	3, 5	6	2, 8	4, 7			
13	1	2	4, 8	5, 7	3	7	6	
14	1	2, 6	5	8	3, 4			9
15	1	3, 4, 5	2, 7		6			8
16	7	3	4	1	2, 5	6		8
17	1	2, 3, 4	6	9	5, 7, 8			10

Passage Number	Finding the Main Idea	Finding Supporting Detail	Making Inferences	Understanding Vocabulary in Context	Drawing Conclusions	Recognizing Style & Tone	Word Problems, Jumbles & Puzzles	DISCUSSION: Thinking About What You Have Read
18	1, 3		2	5	4, 6			7
19	1	5	3	2, 8	4, 6, 7			9, 10
20	2	3, 10	5, 6, 7, 8	1, 4			9	11
21	1	3, 4, 7		2	5, 9	8	6	10, 11
22	1	2, 3	4, 6, 7, 9	8	5		10	
23	1	2, 3	7, 9, 11	6, 10, 13	4, 5, 8	12		
24	2	1, 3, 5, 9	4, 8	6	10	7		11, 12, 13
25	1	3, 5, 8, 9, 10	7	2, 6	4		11	12

TO THE READER: You may wish to use this chart to find out what your reading strengths are. Circle the numbers of the question items you answered correctly. Study the explanations for those questions which you answered incorrectly to increase your skill in those areas.